MASTER *THE* NINE
CYBERSECURITY HABITS
TO PROTECT YOUR FUTURE

WELL AWARE

GEORGE FINNEY

GREENLEAF
BOOK GROUP PRESS

This publication is designed to provide accurate and authoritative information in regard to the subject matter covered. It is sold with the understanding that the publisher and author are not engaged in rendering legal, accounting, or other professional services. Nothing herein shall create an attorney-client relationship, and nothing herein shall constitute legal advice or a solicitation to offer legal advice. If legal advice or other expert assistance is required, the services of a competent professional should be sought.

Published by Greenleaf Book Group Press
Austin, Texas
www.gbgpress.com

Distributed by Greenleaf Book Group

For ordering information or special discounts for bulk purchases, please contact Greenleaf Book Group at PO Box 91869, Austin, TX 78709, 512.891.6100.

Design and composition by Greenleaf Book Group
Cover design by Greenleaf Book Group
Cover Image: ©iStockphoto/hjroy

Publisher's Cataloging-in-Publication data is available.

Print ISBN: 978-1-62634-735-9

eBook ISBN: 978-1-62634-737-3

Audiobook ISBN: 978-1-62634-736-6

Part of the Tree Neutral® program, which offsets the number of trees consumed in the production and printing of this book by taking proactive steps, such as planting trees in direct proportion to the number of trees used: www.treeneutral.com

Printed in the United States of America on acid-free paper

20 21 22 23 24 25   10 9 8 7 6 5 4 3 2 1

First Edition

"Make fear a tailwind instead of a headwind."

—Jimmy Iovine, cofounder, Interscope Records

CONTENTS

FOREWORD

C lose your eyes and think of the word *cybersecurity*. What do you visualize? Nine out of ten people I have asked to conduct this mind exercise have come back with something like "I see a dark room with a number of computers with blinking screens, and someone in a hoodie or sometimes a mask, trying to scramble through some code as if stealing something!" It's a compelling vision of a dark art that is practiced by someone that we refer to by various names: hacker, adversary, threat actor. Seldom do I come across someone who has a more positive vision. And this is the challenge that cybersecurity presents. It appears to be a very bleak and involved topic that only experts can understand and decipher, and we had better leave it to them. And it is this esoteric aspect and a painful absence of simplicity that have gotten us into this challenging circumstance, where we have fewer and fewer experts trying to address an overwhelming amount of challenges.

As the chairman and founder of Cyber Future Foundation (CFF), I have had the opportunity to meet and work with some remarkable leaders around the world. Several executives and prominent global leaders have personally expressed to me a desire to simplify cybersecurity so that they can engage the whole of a nation, enterprise, and society. As we work on the challenging mission of bridging the gap between global leaders and the technically astute and inclined cybersecurity industry and business, we still see cybersecurity challenges being confined to the cybersecurity experts and the industry.

We have to turn this on its head and make cybersecurity a problem that everyone can understand, comprehend, and engage in, not just because we want to get more experts on the subject but because security in cyberspace is everyone's business and responsibility, and without harnessing this collective capacity, we cannot be successful in securing cyberspace, either as individual consumers or as citizens of a connected world, and definitely not as employees of a digital enterprise.

That describes exactly why we need this book by George Finney. Not only is it timely, but I believe it will be timeless in terms of being an objective and compact reference for those who need to understand cybersecurity and how they can make the changes they seek.

In over two decades of a career that has involved cybersecurity through different dimensions, George has been able to see the issues from various perspectives: as an end user, as a technology executive, as an educator, and in his current role as a chief information security officer of a sprawling enterprise.

I have known George for years now, and I have been impressed by his optimistic but realistic approach to issues. His approach to the most technical of challenges is not through the technology but through examining the expectations and outcomes, behavior and results. George has been a steady voice of reason and pragmatism toward addressing the issues of cybersecurity through objective analysis of situations and behaviors, rather than incidents and reactions.

While cybersecurity has its fair share of technological problems and jargons, George brings a very human and relatable approach to studying and learning the topic. Humans are creatures of habits, and it is in this power of habits that George sees the opportunity to advance our learning and engagement as workers, citizens, and consumers and to develop patterns of behaviors that will improve our security posture.

I believe as the reader goes through this book, they will be enlightened by how everyone can get engaged in cybersecurity by following the habits that George lays out. The concepts are supported by the brilliant recollection of anecdotes, events, and incidents, which makes it abundantly easier on the reader to embrace them. I believe through this book that the reader will become intimately familiar with their role in securing their journey, embrace security as a behavior, and be able to actively contribute in securing our digital life.

As a cybersecurity professional, as a business leader, and definitely as a parent, this book has been a validation of my thoughts. With George's book as a reference, a lot of the work we are doing at CFF— whether the executive engagement at the Cyber Future Dialogue in Davos or the engagement of young cybersecurity professionals through the CFF Society of Mentors—becomes a tad bit easier. Next time someone has a recollection of the bleak vision of cybersecurity— of a teenager in a hoodie in their mom's basement hacking away at networks—a definite action is going to be referring them to the positive, uplifting, and engaging story of the Girl Scouts and their keen enthusiasm in earning cybersecurity merit badges.

The world we live in is becoming more connected and is rapidly changing to where we need to understand what ties it all together and how we can keep it safe and secure. George has done his part, and now it is up to us to take the lessons from this book and change our behavior. As we say at CFF, let's work to build a more trusted cyberspace—the much-needed help is here!

—**Valmiki Mukherjee**
Chairman and Founder, Cyber Future Foundation
Chairman and Convener, Cyber Future Dialogue, Davos, Switzerland
Convener, Cyber 20 Engagement Group for G20 Heads of States
www.cyberfuturefoundation.org

INTRODUCTION—
THE NINE
CYBERSECURITY HABITS

I'd like to tell you a story about an entrepreneur named Johann. Johann built an invention he thought would change the world. He convinced a venture capitalist (VC) to invest $100,000 in his business so he could create a prototype. With the funding secured, Johann hired employees and began to train his staff on how to use the invention.

Two years later, just as the invention was perfected, the VC sued Johann. The VC claimed that he hadn't invested in the company but instead had provided Johann a loan, and the loan was now overdue. Johann, who could not find his partnership agreement documents, provided no evidence at trial, and the court sided with the VC, awarding him the invention and the business. Johann was left penniless.

Unbeknownst to Johann, his company had been the victim of a rogue insider. Johann's most trusted employee, a man named Peter, had been recruited by the VC. In the beginning, the VC insisted that Johann hire Peter, who would eventually become the VC's son-in-law. In exchange for inside information, the VC promised to make Peter the CEO of the company once it had been swindled from Johann. Peter routinely fed financial information and trade secrets to the VC and eventually found and destroyed Johann's partnership agreement documents. Then the VC went in for the kill.

Johann died about a decade after he lost his business, largely an unknown figure. His company, led by Peter and the VC, could not compete with the flood of competition that had entered the marketplace after their hostile takeover—they were not innovators like Johann was.

The year was 1456. Johann's last name was Gutenberg. And his invention was the printing press. Gutenberg's introduction of mechanical type started the printing revolution and is regarded today as a milestone of the second millennium, ushering in the modern era of human history.

I often wonder what other world-changing innovations Gutenberg would have given us if only he had had better security. We can learn a lot from this story because we face the same problems today that Gutenberg faced six hundred years ago—though we've come a long way in regard to technology and security risks.

Today, every company in the world is now a technology company with a presence on the internet, using computers and the cloud to make their businesses more efficient and profitable. Families use the wonders of the internet to make their lives richer. Technology brings communities together in ways that weren't possible twenty years ago.

But the internet is both one of the wonders of the world and the bad side of town where you lock your car doors and hope your vehicle doesn't break down. With this new reality comes the potential for crime to happen on a scale never possible before. With so much of our information being stored on the internet, families, communities, and businesses are susceptible to its dark side: Criminals can reach into our homes and bank accounts, and governments around the globe can read our email and listen to our most private conversations. We must learn to protect ourselves from these threats, and protecting ourselves is an instinct we are all born with.

Security is part of our DNA

As social animals, humans have evolved to form, travel in, and live in groups. Humans do this not because they necessarily like each other but for their collective protection. Security is part of our DNA. A single human is a weak animal compared to some of the predators roaming the planet. As a group, however, humans are the most formidable species to have ever existed. But there is a big exception to this rule when it comes to computers and the internet. While we humans have had the benefit of millennia to recognize dangers in the world around us, we've only had about thirty years to practice recognizing and stopping threats in cyberspace, and we have a lot to learn.

Unfortunately, a lot of people and businesses don't realize just how important security is. To some, security seems like a waste of money. They say, "If only we didn't need to spend money on security, we would be more profitable and could spend more time doing the things we love." Early in my career, I heard a leader in my company say, "Don't let security get in the way of employees doing their jobs." Many in the security community attempt to overcome this kind of objection to investing in security by using fear or by leveraging compliance to get things done. Compliance isn't security. Even if you do achieve the elusive goal of compliance, there is no reason left to invest in security. When the right kind of protection isn't employed, the door for enormous risk opens. And interestingly enough, over the past several years, I've seen more and more CEOs being fired for failing to protect their companies. Security is everyone's job.

I'm not telling you these things to scare you. This book isn't about fear. Instead, this book will show you how you can be confident (but not overconfident) and even optimistic (but not naïve) about security. We are optimistic because failure isn't an option. Optimism is a prerequisite for success. Moreover, as we'll see in some of the stories that follow, cybersecurity is a competitive advantage that has helped some companies become leaders in their industries.

I've written this book to help you—whether at work, at home, or in your community—translate the security DNA built into every one of us into the cybersecurity world. To do that, I'll share some of the lessons I've learned in my twenty years of experience helping companies defend against hackers. Today, I am a chief information security officer for a major university, but in my career, I've been a consultant for telecommunications firms, health-care organizations, financial institutions, and nonprofits, helping them to build and mature their security programs. I've also advised startup organizations who know that to be successful they need to think about cybersecurity before they've hired their first employee. And I've worked with individuals who've been affected by ransomware or identity theft to establish stronger cyber hygiene and get back to living their lives. And throughout the book, I won't just share my experiences; I'll also share stories from some of the leading cybersecurity experts in the world about how they've learned to protect themselves and their organizations.

Security is about people

Security professionals will tell you there are three parts to security: people, processes, and technology. But people are the ones who write and employ processes. People are the ones who create and use technology. It shouldn't be surprising to learn, then, that people are the cause of nearly 95 percent of all cybersecurity incidents, according to a recent *Verizon Data Breach Report*.[1] I would go further and say that people are the cause of 100 percent of cybersecurity breaches. These statistics have led many security practitioners to want to write off people as the weakest link in security. I would argue that people are the *only* link in security. And if there were a way to improve human security, even by just a small amount, say 20 percent to 30 percent, the outlook for the cybersecurity world could be radically changed.

Security is a people problem, and people can become adept at cybersecurity by implementing certain habits and behaviors. It follows then that when it comes to the security of the information we store on our computers at our businesses or when we are using social media or shopping online, we need to consider lessons on protection, not only from computer programmers but also from neuroscientists and psychologists.

And corporations need to use the evolving sciences of behavioral economics and human learning to change the way their employees interact through the mediums of computers, email, and networks.

I've been part of numerous emergency operations activities, both tabletop exercises and responses to the real thing. I've worked with the Federal Bureau of Investigation and Secret Service to prepare for emergency response activities. One of the common themes that every trainer talks about is that you must be prepared to expect some degree of diminished mental capacity in stressful situations, both in yourself and in the people around you. Sometimes communication will fail because of lack of sleep. Sometimes, an overwhelming amount of stress can shut down a person's capacity to solve problems as quickly as they would otherwise.[2] Sometimes fear will cause people to point blame, deflecting attention away from themselves. This is precisely the opposite of what needs to happen most. Being prepared for an emergency situation helps, but if an organization or family can come together in that moment and live up to their potential, they can not only survive it but also become better as a part of the process.

This observation is where the nine cybersecurity habits started to crystallize for me. The field of psychology went through a revolution starting in the 1950s; instead of exclusively studying dysfunctional people, researchers began to study happy, well-adjusted people. This change has been transformational because it focuses on behaviors that allow humans to thrive, despite their circumstances. Cybersecurity today focuses on the dysfunction—we study what people do wrong in order to avoid their mistakes rather than what people do right. Traditional security training only focuses on informing people: providing best practices, laying out guidelines, and detailing compliance requirements. The traditional approach to training doesn't address how people make the choices they do, nor does it address why they make those decisions.

This is one of the most important insights that I can provide: As humans, we have the unique ability to understand how our own minds work, and then we can change our own minds from the outside in. As you will read in the coming chapters, when we apply this concept to cybersecurity, we must understand not only the technical aspects of security but also the psychology and neuroscience behind it. Security is not a competency; it is a behavior. Behaviors can't be changed overnight, but they can be changed. Mark Twain wrote that habits can't be thrown out the window but must be coaxed downstairs one step at a time.[3] This book will attempt to coax these security habits out into the open for everyone to benefit from.

I recently interviewed a manager about his department's cybersecurity practices. I asked him whether they locked their paper records up at night. He said yes, they always kept their files locked, not just at night. I pointed to the filing cabinet in his office, where the key was still sticking out of the lock, and asked, "Do you ever take the key out?"

Uncomfortable silence.

If you only take one thing away from this book, it should be this: Cybersecurity is a behavior, not a skill. For years, we've taught cybersecurity awareness as though it were a skill to be learned like any other technology. People are smart; they've listened to the training. And when you ask them questions about cybersecurity, they know the right answers. However, when you inquire whether they're implementing the knowledge and skills, you discover that they aren't.

If you've ever gotten advice on your golf swing, you know that keeping all of those little tidbits of knowledge in your head while you're holding a club can be a challenge. Keep your knees bent. Breathe. Hold your club like this. Bend your elbows. Eye on the ball. Follow through. Security awareness has failed because we aren't looking at modifying or influencing behaviors; we're just giving tidbits of advice without a strategy for getting people to put them into practice.

But what behaviors need to change? If you do a quick internet search, you'll find that lists of cybersecurity tips include all kinds of specific things people can do to be more cybersecure, but it's not realistic to expect people to memorize every one. Even if they did, when a new variation of social engineering comes along, they still wouldn't be prepared.

What we need, then, is an understanding of the underlying structures that govern a person's choices and help them make the right decisions. After years of teaching cybersecurity, I realized that all of the tips or advice we give on how to be secure fall into several different categories. This brought me to my next realization: Security isn't just one monolithic set of behaviors that can be changed. As I explored these categories, I understood that these weren't just categories; they were habits. There are nine different cybersecurity habits, and they all build on one another like the rungs of a ladder. You can still use the ladder even if an individual rung on the ladder is weak, or even missing. But the stronger the ladder, the greater the heights that can be safely reached. In the chapters that follow, I'll describe how we'll use these nine habits to change behaviors and then measure that change.

- **Literacy**—An element of security involves understanding your environment. This involves continuous learning. You need to know how your alarm system works, how to set privacy settings, and what kinds of scams to be on the lookout for. Literacy also means being aware and making informed decisions.

- **Skepticism**—My wife is from Missouri, which calls itself the "Show Me State" because residents won't believe anything unless they see it with their own eyes. Being a skeptic means not trusting something until you've established its credibility, which also requires patience.

- **Vigilance**—This state of mind is about keeping watch so that when you see something, you are ready to recognize it and act. Monitoring server logs and reviewing physical access records are great examples of this. Vigilance is a kind of directed skepticism toward specific threats.

- **Secrecy**—Secrecy is the natural barrier between that which is public and that which is private. This barrier is a healthy part of every human experience. It is so integral to our society that it is a guaranteed protection in the US Constitution's Bill of Rights. The controls we use to protect ourselves are dictated by the nature of the secrets that require protection.

- **Culture**—Security controls in and of themselves are not enough for protection. When groups of people form, norms are established. Sometimes, these norms are antithetical to security. In these cases, one person changing their behavior won't change the whole company. A culture of cybersecurity embraced at all levels of a company, government, or community is needed.

- **Diligence**—Once you've developed security routines, you need to have a plan for orchestrating how those routines work together. After you've experienced an incident, you must have plans and protocols for handling the way you respond.

- **Community**—You need help to be secure. We work together to solve problems. We share information to protect others and unite in a common defense. We must look for help not just from law enforcement or inside our companies but from peers in our industry or in similar roles across industries.

- **Mirroring**—An element of curiosity is involved in mirroring. You want to be able to see yourself and what you look like from someone else's perspective. Penetration testing is this habit put into practice, but so is looking at your social media profiles from different perspectives or googling your own name.

- **Deception**—Have you ever seen a movie where someone asks a question like "Do you know Captain Harris?" When the person answers, "Yes, of course!" you know they're lying because Captain Harris doesn't exist. You might create "lies" you use for common password challenge questions. Or you might set up a "honeypot" or a security mechanism on your internal network to alert you if anyone accesses it. Deception can be both a preventive and detective habit.

Each of these nine cybersecurity habits builds on the previous to form a shield you can use to protect yourself, your organization, or your community. To protect yourself, you need to be security literate. You need to understand your environment and know how to protect yourself online. The internet is always evolving, so to stay literate, you must continually relearn your environment. And you must understand the best way to educate yourself, your family, or your business.

Staying literate requires skepticism because you shouldn't always believe what you read. Skepticism requires vigilance because you must be able to recognize when something is suspicious. Vigilance requires secrecy because you must know what to protect and how to protect it. Secrecy requires culture because protecting things means following a regular pattern of protective behaviors. Culture requires diligence because you must have a plan for coordinating all of these protective behaviors. Diligence requires community because you won't be able to protect yourself alone. Community requires mirroring because once you start working with other people, you need to understand what information you share with others and how you do it. Mirroring requires deception since how much you trust an outsider will be limited, and you must know how to conceal private information.

When a company experiences a breach due to a failure of the "human element," it's because one or more of these layers of the shield was weak or missing. Let's look at phishing as an example. Phishing is a type of email message that attempts to trick you into clicking on a link to get you to give away your password or go to a website that will install malware on your computer. If an employee knew they clicked on a phishing link (vigilance, skepticism) but didn't report it (community, diligence) and didn't change their password afterward (culture), then improving just one of those habits could have stopped that click. To successfully improve our cybersecurity, we must get people to take the keys out of the filing cabinet—to replace their old habits with new, better ones.

These nine habits are just as relevant for the programmer coding the next great app as they are for the soccer mom who just wants to protect her kids online. They are just as relevant for the former law enforcement computer forensics investigator as they are for the business executive who is moving his organization into the digital age.

Security is not a technology problem. Sometimes, people make the mistake of believing technology is the most important part of any security program. It isn't. People are the most important part. People use the technology, and people create and implement the processes. This book will focus on how people think and behave when it comes to cybersecurity. To be successful, you can't simply be reactive to threats in your environment. This book will help you identify and proactively change the behaviors that most commonly lead to security challenges, before you've been hacked or breached. To do this, we'll look at leaders who exemplify the nine cybersecurity habits and how they used those habits to make their own organizations both more secure and more successful.

1

LITERACY

When I inherited the security program at Southern Methodist University (SMU) in Dallas, Texas, I had a problem. The IT department had been doing security training for years. Some training materials had been developed, mostly as a handful of PowerPoint slides. Our trainer emailed them to me, obviously relieved to not have to do this anymore, and said, "It's your job now!" Where did I need to begin? What did I need to train people on? What did they need to know?

I had been doing cybersecurity for years—hardening servers or configuring firewalls—but your average person doesn't need to know all of the technical details about security. And unfortunately, at first, rather than figuring out the foundation of knowledge that I needed to provide, I focused on the details. When it became common for employees to carry smartphones, my team and I focused on how to secure those devices. When ransomware rose in popularity, we educated users about what it is and how to avoid it. As phishing continued to rise, we began using simulated phishing campaigns to teach about recognizing such messages. After years of this, I realized we were just plugging our fingers into the holes of the dam. This was the wrong approach. What we had been doing was giving people fish instead of teaching them to fish. Instead, we needed to understand what a foundation for security might look like. So, I tried to figure out what cybersecurity awareness was and how I could make people cybersecurity literate without forcing them to become firewall engineers along the way.

If you were to ask someone what it meant to be literate, they would say that you should be able to recognize the words on a page. You can be fluent in spoken English but still be illiterate if you can't read the words and write them down. I think the definition of cybersecurity literacy should follow this model. You don't need to know everything there is to know about cybersecurity to be considered literate. But you do need to be able to recognize the words on the page. You need a proper foundation so you can ask the right questions and know where to get answers to those questions. This foundation is built by optimizing cybersecurity education, building awareness, understanding tactical literacy, having an adaptable framework in place, and securing the brain.

Fearless learning

In June 2017, I was in Vancouver, British Columbia, attending Palo Alto Networks' annual cybersecurity conference, Ignite. Typically, the focus is on in-depth technical challenges and on how customers are solving those problems using Palo Alto's technology, but something different happened in 2017. During the opening keynote, Mark McLaughlin, who was the CEO of Palo Alto Networks at the time, stepped aside and welcomed the Girl Scouts CEO, Sylvia Acevedo. Acevedo came onstage and announced that her organization had partnered with Palo Alto Networks to create a series of cybersecurity-focused merit badges for girls.

Acevedo had been on the board of the Girl Scouts for eight years when she was asked to become the interim CEO in June 2016. At the time, the Girl Scouts were in the planning stages of completely revamping their merit badges to incorporate science, technology, engineering, and math (STEM) and other important concepts. Through surveys across the country, they asked girls what they were interested in, and girls of all ages answered that they wanted to learn about one topic: cybersecurity.

In 2016 TechCrunch reported that the average girl gets a smartphone at age ten.[1] By that age, many children already have email addresses necessitated by their school or other activities. The Girl Scouts realized that girls didn't have a trusted source for information on how to protect themselves in a digital world. They realized they had a calling to fill that gap. But what would be the best method to teach these girls about cybersecurity?

The real challenge for Acevedo was figuring out how to teach girls about something as complicated as cybersecurity. The answer, as it turns out, doesn't just apply to Brownies or Daisies. The answer applies equally well to dentists or CEOs. To teach someone, you need to figure out what interests them and what is relevant, and then you need to find a way to make that knowledge practical.

Acevedo began her career as a rocket scientist at NASA's Jet Propulsion Laboratory, where she worked on NASA's Voyager 2 mission.[2] She has held executive and engineering roles at leading technology companies, such as Apple, Dell, Autodesk Inc., and IBM. Acevedo's background in technology led her to ask the following questions: What if we adopt agile development methods and apply them to the merit badge process? How can we short-circuit the development process and get girls the skills they need when they need them?

In technology, the concept of agile development began to gain momentum in the early 2000s.[3] Modern software can include billions of lines of code. So, it's important to make sure that the code, as written, actually does what the users, customers, and businesses need it to do. Old development methods were like those used to build a building: An architect came up with the plans, and the builder delivered on those plans. Unlike with a building, if the software wasn't right at the end of the project, it would usually get thrown away, and the process would start over. Agile development is different in that it gives the users, customers, and executives a chance to provide feedback while the building is being built. This process requires developers to break projects down into small, individual pieces. They use "sprints" to deliver these pieces quickly, usually within two to three weeks instead of the years or decades it normally takes to build software. This is why companies like Google now deliver their software with "beta" on them; being in beta means that the software is still being tested and new features will continue to roll out much more rapidly than they otherwise would.

In applying this agile method of development, the Girl Scouts looked to partners like Palo Alto Networks for subject matter experts in different areas. Finding the core subjects in a field helped define what needed to be taught. The Girl Scouts then applied their understanding of how girls learn to come up with the programs and activities for how to teach these subjects in each age group. They continue to test these teaching methods to find out what works best and to make sure the activities are fun and relevant, ensuring the girls want to keep learning. The security strategy that fits your needs might be different depending on who you are: A recent college graduate looking for a job needs different strategies to stay secure than a vice president who is looking to become a CEO. A one-size-fits-all approach won't meet either person's needs, so it's best to experiment rapidly to see what doesn't work and what leads to success.

In the Girl Scouts, girls are grouped by age. Grouping the girls this way is important to learning because each age defines a new stage of development, and education is tailored to each stage. To teach coding to Daisies (grades K-1), you need to show how computers talk to one another in binary language. Computers transmit code in bits that are labeled as a zero or a one. Computers string millions of these ones and zeros together every second as they talk to one another. But you'll lose the Daisies if you talk about ones and zeros. Instead, the Girl Scouts put blue and yellow beads on the table. Then, they have the alphabet expressed not as zeros and ones but as yellow and blue. The Daisies are asked to write their initials on a bracelet using the code. What happens after this is amazing. The girls come back wanting a longer piece of string.

They want to write not just their initials but their whole name. Then they come back and ask for an even longer piece of string because they want to write all their names together. "You've taught them an unbelievably complex idea in a way that they can wrap their heads around," said Sapreet Saluja, chief strategic partnerships and new ventures officer for the Girl Scouts. "And then they build on it and build on that. And then by the time they're ready to learn the next skill, they get it practically, and they know how to build from there. Not only do we, per our mission, want them to use those skills to impact the world, but it's also what they want. It's one of the most important things to them. It ends up being the delta between interest and disinterest if there is something practical they can do with their knowledge."

To teach Brownies (grades 2-3) about important concepts in cybersecurity like networking and malware, where would you begin? You can't start by describing how TCP/IP protocols encapsulate data into headers. You can't teach them the OSI seven-layer model of networking. Instead, the Girl Scouts teach the importance of a physical network in transmitting computer viruses to someone the girls have never connected with. The Brownies sit in a circle and pass a ball of yarn to one another; in a short amount of time, a physical network appears. Then they can show how Alice talked to Jane and then Sara talked to Jane. They can see in the network how the malware was transmitted from Alice to Sara. This is relevant to the girls not just because they start to see a pattern emerge but because while they're doing it, they're constantly reinforcing the things most important to the girls: community and connection. But how do we apply this agile development model of learning to help others learn about cybersecurity?

When I began running the training program at SMU, we trained our employees about cybersecurity exclusively through yearly in-person sessions. At the time, we typically only reached about 5 percent of our total workforce each year using this method. One session, for which I had spent months developing the content and rehearsing, only had two people show up. We offered free drinks, popcorn, and prizes to encourage people to come. But our outreach efforts were always limited because our staff was too busy doing their day-to-day work. Our most successful outreach came from going to departmental meetings where we would talk about relevant security issues for twenty to thirty minutes, but those opportunities were rare.

Before I go too much further, I should acknowledge that the goal of training isn't efficiency. It's tempting to say that in-person training was a waste of time. The goal of training is to help employees or family members understand security and make better decisions based on this understanding. When we were able to train one-on-one at SMU, we found that one of the biggest benefits of this approach was the relationships we built along the way. Even if the message wasn't clearly understood, everyone knew whom to call when a problem came up. These meetings established enough trust that they were comfortable sharing those problems with us. And as you will see, this in itself is a very important part of cybersecurity literacy.

Next, I adopted a hybrid approach: We still met with departments about cybersecurity to continue the dialogue we had already begun, but we switched our main outreach method to an online class. We were able to drastically increase our outreach. We went from reaching 5 percent of our users to reaching nearly 20 percent. Employees who couldn't get away from their desks could now take our training whenever they were able. The training program wasn't mandatory at this point, but this was a huge success.

A lot of companies provide online security awareness training. A company called Cybrary offers free security awareness classes, but other excellent training is available from the SANS Institute, KnowBe4, Proofpoint, MediaPRO, and others. Compliance regimes now recommend some form of training, and programs like this will check the box of security awareness training. But checking a box doesn't create security literacy. Often, these programs operate more like sexual harassment or diversity training—the same courses are offered year after year. People see them as a waste of time and make fun of them. They try to cheat to skip ahead or just leave the mandatory video playing while they walk away for a meeting. These programs aren't customized for individuals, and they don't consider what that person might already know. They aren't progressive. In a college course, you would take a 101 class your freshman year, then a 202 class your sophomore year, and so on. You learn concepts, and then you build on those concepts, progressing to a more advanced level.

This isn't a book about metrics, but it's tempting to look at the percentages above as a reflection of the effectiveness of our security program. I certainly focused far too much on the numbers. It's easy to focus on percentages when they aren't very high, but these numbers fall short of telling the whole story. Our 20 percent outreach was good for a voluntary program but not great in the larger scheme of things. This didn't mean we weren't secure or didn't have a culture that valued security. We would later make annual training mandatory. At that point, we consistently got above 95 percent participation, but this number still does not reflect the effectiveness of our security training efforts. The number of users trained isn't a success metric. Some training programs require a quiz before and after the training session, but that doesn't reflect the success of training efforts either—that is more like teaching to the test.

What I've realized is that the way to measure the effectiveness of training, and thereby help create cybersecurity literacy, is to measure the outcomes of that training. Have your behaviors changed? Has the success of phishing campaigns been diminished? Do employees engage in less risky behavior? Has the number of breaches or incidents dropped because employees are more secure? Or has the number of breaches or incidents increased due to a higher awareness of issues and reporting? Are we still building relationships so people will call us when there is a problem? Or are we harming those relationships because people resent us for wasting their time?

Without a way of measuring global outcomes, we can't evaluate which training method for an individual is most effective. We can't measure which training session had the biggest impact. We can't know which security training vendor has the right courses that will work for each person.

The other mistake I made in developing a security awareness training program was that I only considered the program one class at a time. I didn't consider each individual's training needs. If you are educating your employees to be literate in cybersecurity, you must first assess what the relevant individuals' learning styles are and how you can customize the material to meet their needs. Consider where an employee is in terms of their security maturity—what courses have they already taken and what good habits do they already have? Think about their role and how they perform their duties. How much access to sensitive information do they have? How much or how little do they use technology? How computer literate are they already? By knowing the answers to these questions, you can tailor education to your employees.

In marketing, they use "personas" to understand who their audience is before developing a campaign for them, and in security, this is also crucial. When I create training materials, I use several security personas based on the level of access for each person and how they use technology. Using these personas helps me understand the needs, motivations, pain points, and communication styles for each and allows me to meet employees where they are to connect with them rather than expect them to connect with me. A good persona includes a photo, a name, demographics, motivations, quotes, and more.

Users who telecommute or travel frequently for work might have time constraints or limitations on how and when they can receive training. Users who primarily use mobile devices might have more limited access with which to receive training. Telecommuters should be very knowledgeable about virtual private networks, while mobile users might need more device-specific policies and procedures for how to access information. But the final dilemma is how to measure whether your efforts have been effective and to further improve them based on reaching the desired outcome: changing behaviors.

The nine habits presented in this book are my answer to this dilemma. Each habit is a measurement of a dimension of security outcomes. Each can be measured, just like high blood pressure, cholesterol, daily caloric intake, or daily exercise rates. This provides a more global picture for an organization, but it also gives us a detailed picture of an individual. The same training course for one person won't be as effective for someone else in a different job or with a different personal history or learning style. Once you have a way to educate in place, you need to build awareness of what we are trying to protect and from whom.

Unfortunately, learning can be scary. One group suggests that up to 38 percent of the population has moderate to severe test anxiety.[4] I met the founder of Monster.com, Jeff Taylor, at a conference early in my career. I vividly remember one of the pieces of advice that he gave. He said, "If you're nervous, you're in danger of learning something." Taylor observed that most people do the same thing every day; new experiences can, consequently, make them nervous. Instead of being afraid of these experiences, we should seek them out like explorers.

The challenges girls face with cybersecurity are the same ones we all face. We're isolated from one another, afraid or embarrassed to talk about our security failures. We've been conditioned to believe that loose lips sink ships. In the past, cybersecurity leaders and vendors grabbed short-term attention or increases in budget by using fear, uncertainty, and doubt (FUD). The Girl Scouts offer an alternative to everyone: fearless learning. They hear from the girls that they are having fun while doing these activities and making connections with other girls—that is meaningful. Learning requires a safe environment and a patient mentor willing to allow individuals to go through the process of self-discovery and learn from their own mistakes along the way. When learning is fun, you want to keep doing it. "We don't lead through fear," Girl Scouts' Acevedo said. "We are raising girls to be courageous, confident people. We're giving them the skills to be fearless."

Self-awareness

Just outside of Albany, New York, in a wooded office park, is the headquarters of one of the most well-regarded security organizations in the world: the Center for Internet Security (CIS). The CIS provides a wealth of resources to the global community of security professionals, most of which are free. Each year, the CIS produces its Controls for Effective Cyber Defense (CIS Controls).[5] The CIS Controls is "a relatively short list of high-priority, highly effective defensive actions that provide a 'must-do, do-first' starting point for every enterprise seeking to improve their cyber defense." Every year, one recommendation is always at the very top of the list: Build an inventory. I think of this inventory as creating a kind of treasure map showing where the crown jewels are buried. Without a map, you can't protect yourself or your company.

Knowing yourself is one of the primary aspects of cybersecurity literacy. What information do you have in your possession, and are those records in electronic or paper form? What systems do you have access to, and how much access do you have? What does your online presence look like? What banking or email or social media accounts do you have? Have you googled yourself or checked to see what your social media accounts look like to a stranger? Have you set up alerts to notify you when your email address or phone number or company name appears online?

Once you have begun to "know thyself" (what you need to protect), the next step is to know your enemy. You need to be aware of the potential threats and what to look out for. In cybersecurity terms, knowing your enemy means understanding the cyber kill chain. The kill chain is a military concept that Lockheed Martin recently adapted to the world of information security so that it could better understand how hackers were targeting its information. The company broke down the original four steps of the military kill chain into seven stages: reconnaissance, weaponization, delivery, exploitation, installation, command and control, and actions or objectives.[6] Cyber reconnaissance may come in the form of monitoring LinkedIn profiles of a company's employees or harvesting data from a corporate website. Next, hackers will choose an exploit, a method that takes advantage of a particular vulnerability, that suits the target and then put this exploit into a package. The first two steps in the chain can take an attacker from hours to months of preparation and planning.

In the second phase (stages three through five of the kill chain), which can take just seconds, the package is delivered to the target via email or an infected USB stick, which, in the delivery stage, is shipped to the victim. In the USB scenario, this might mean the hacker leaves a bunch of infected USB devices in the parking lot for unsuspecting victims to find or mails them to specific victims as though they were a gift from a vendor. Once the package is run, the code is executed, and malware is installed on the target. In this case, the target could be a laptop, mobile phone, desktop, or server. In the third and final phase (stages six and seven), the goals of the attack are reached in a breach. The computer joins a command-and-control network to receive additional instructions and additional attack payloads. The attacks achieve their objectives, like exfiltrating or destroying data, holding a victim hostage, or stealing secrets for a competitive advantage.

As Sun Tzu wrote,

"If you know the enemy and know yourself, you need not fear the result of a hundred battles."

If you know that your enemy needs to do reconnaissance before performing an attack, you can be prepared to disrupt that step of the kill chain. While you may not know where every attack will come from, if you know yourself and what and where your crown jewels are, you can anticipate where your adversaries are going and stop them from getting there. You can monitor for connections to a command-and-control network to give you a heads-up that you've been compromised so you can act to prevent information from being compromised further. This can be done by reviewing previous login attempts manually or by looking at network logs with an automated tool. Sometimes an "air gap" that requires a person to manually review a transaction before a check is written is enough to prevent an exploit from happening. There isn't a single perfect method, but the more creative and tailored an approach you take, the better your chances are to disrupt an attack.

Unfortunately, there is also a risk in knowing too much.

Tactical literacy

Twenty-five hundred years ago, there was a prophecy about the smartest person in the world. In ancient Greece, a priestess inside the Temple of Apollo at Delphi was the Pythia—more commonly known as the Oracle at Delphi. Two young men entered the Oracle's temple. One asked whether anyone in the world was smarter than his friend. The priestess replied that no one was wiser.[7] The philosopher Plato would discuss this man's life and conversations with other famous men extensively in his *Dialogues*. The man's name was Socrates.

I can't imagine the pressure Socrates would have been under if this story is true. Socrates responded to the prophecy by spending the rest of his life attempting to prove it wrong. In one of his most famous dialogues, he said, "God only is wise; and in this oracle he means to say that the wisdom of men is little or nothing," the lesson being that Socrates was the wisest person in the world precisely because he knew that whatever knowledge he thought he possessed was meaningless.

The most dominant chess player in the history of the game was a German named Emanuel Lasker, who held the World Chess Champion title from 1894 to 1921—an unprecedented twenty-seven years. For comparison purposes, Garry Kasparov held the title for only fifteen years; Bobby Fischer was champion for only three. In addition to his chess genius, Lasker was also a philosopher, mathematician, and prolific author. Despite this, Lasker took pains to ensure he only ever remembered the few things he needed to know rather than striving for perfect recall. At the end of his life, he was quoted as saying, "Of my 57 years, I have applied at least 30 to forgetting most of what I have learned or read . . . I have stored little in my memory, but I can apply that little. I keep it in order but resist every attempt to increase its dead weight."[8]

The common thread between Socrates and Lasker is that they didn't place value on knowledge or facts. What made them both so impactful on the world around them was that they had a system or framework that guided how they applied their understanding to the world around them.

If the Girl Scouts provide an understanding of how we can learn, Socrates and Lasker provide a clue to when we should be learning. It's not what you know about cybersecurity that matters so much as it's your commitment to learning new things just at the time you need to know them. Socrates always asked questions, tore down old ideas, and proposed new ones. This method of challenging the status quo is such an effective way of learning that it has a name, the Socratic method. Nearly every law school in the country uses this method to teach budding lawyers not just to memorize facts about the law but how to think on their feet.

This is just as true twenty-five hundred years later when we think of cybersecurity. We can never know enough, and what we do know is useless moments after we learn it. Computer systems are constantly being changed or updated, and hackers are constantly evolving their attacks as companies and individuals update their defenses. Studying the malware from thirty years ago provides only limited value to protecting ourselves today. Instead, what we need, like Lasker, is a framework to learn what we need to know when we need to know it. What we need is tactical literacy.

In 1990 Stanford psychology graduate student Elizabeth Newton conducted an experiment. She asked one group of subjects to tap out the tune to several of their favorite songs. Other subjects were asked to listen to the tapping and guess what song the other subject was tapping. The tapper was asked to estimate how many of the listeners would be able to guess the song. The tapper would always vastly overestimate the number of people who would recognize the song.[9]

This phenomenon, known in psychology circles as the curse of knowledge, is true for any area or discipline where an individual gains expertise in a specific subject. They expect others around them to have the same background for understanding the things they have become an expert in. Try this experiment at your next meeting or social gathering. I've personally recreated this experiment, and it's still shocking to me, even though I'm aware of the curse of knowledge. In my own unscientific experiments, only about 5 percent of people correctly guess the tune of "Twinkle, Twinkle Little Star."

This curse of knowledge also applies to cybersecurity. Most cybersecurity training, books, or courses attempt to turn people into cybersecurity practitioners, not more secure versions of the human resources professionals or accountants or attorneys that they already are.

Several years ago, I taught an introduction to cybersecurity course at Southern Methodist University. One of my challenges with the course was that, since it was an introduction to cybersecurity, none of the students had a background in the subject. Some had taken classes on writing software, but they didn't have a background in computer networks. The class was about how to provide defensive cybersecurity for corporations, and I found that the way the textbook explained some of the most fundamental concepts, like encryption, was impossible for a layperson to understand. I tried to use analogies and break down the confusing jargon into plain English, but sometimes I would look out from the whiteboard to see blank stares looking back at me. In some lessons, I would find myself having to explain three other fundamental concepts before I could get back to the original point I needed to make.

This is the problem that tactical literacy addresses. When you need to know something, you will often discover a vast amount of other knowledge along the way to learning what you were hoping to understand. Memorizing all of this extraneous data will not help you retain the answer to the question you originally asked. Tactical literacy involves two things: creating a foundation and knowing when and how to get additional information. But how do you know what information is important and what is extraneous?

One of the most grueling aspects of the first year of law school, already one of the most demanding years of higher education I've made it through, is legal writing. At the end of the year, law students all over the country are asked to perform real research on a hypothetical scenario. In my class, we were forbidden from using the computer to assist with this research, which meant hunting through the library for weeks to find all of the relevant cases on the topic. I knew I was finally nearing the end of my research when the same few cases kept coming back up with every new line of research I tried.

Cybersecurity literacy comes when you know how, where, and when to look for the answer to a problem and when you recognize the solution. But the real challenge is avoiding the cognitive bias that will encourage you to assume that you already have everything you need.

Humans need to understand the risks involved in the activities that they undertake. A doctor and a lawyer may have very different needs regarding understanding security. They collect different types of information, and we expect that much of what is shared by a patient or a client will be kept anonymous or confidential. But doctors and lawyers don't need to know everything in advance about every security defense out there. They need to know only what is relevant to their specific environment at that moment in time. If a new electronic health record system is being rolled out, a doctor must become familiar with a specific set of topics and tasks. An attorney taking on an unpopular figure in a controversial trial will need to prepare differently than the doctor.

One of the challenges with security awareness training is that the security professionals doing the training tend to want to make the employees into other security professionals. Does a mother of four need to understand the difference between a stateless firewall and a stateful firewall? No. But she does need to know about security and privacy on a smartphone when her kids ask for one for their birthday. She will need to be able to lock down her computer and internet connection when her children are given access to websites to ensure they see age-appropriate content.

An adaptable framework

There is a saying at NASA: "No matter how bad the situation is, you can always make it worse." This saying isn't meant to place blame on a single person but to remind them they have a team on the ground to support them; they don't have to do everything themselves. In his book, *Spaceman*, about the greatest astronauts in history, Mike Massimino writes, "The difficulty of our present moment should inspire us, not discourage us."[10] He wrote this about the future of the space program, but the same can be said of improving cybersecurity. If we can put people in space with the processing power of a smartphone, we can help create a culture of security that empowers people to protect themselves and the people around them. To make informed risk decisions, individuals must habitually obtain relevant information related to cybersecurity. The problem is that it's very difficult to know what information you need and even more difficult to observe how this information is relevant to every aspect of your daily life or your business from sales to payroll. That's why it's so important that we have a framework for defense in place that is adaptable.

We'll examine this concept more closely in Chapter 7 when we explore the community habit, but to establish a framework that you can implement, the solution is to find a cybersecurity coach or mentor. If you're a small company, you might need a consultant to shepherd you through—something between an executive coach and a law firm. If you're a large company, you may need a full-time chief security officer who understands your business as well as any other executive in your organization and who can work with everyone to bake security into each layer of the company. Usually individuals will ask a family member or a close friend for assistance, and when all else fails, they might ask a particularly knowledgeable fourteen-year-old. These coaches will change depending on your circumstances, but here are some issues a cybersecurity coach might help walk you through:

- **Who you gonna call?** Find out which person you should contact during an incident. For personal incidents, bookmark the Federal Trade Commission's privacy quick reference page to know what your liability is if your credit card or banking info is lost.[11]

- **What are the rules?** Even if you don't read every word, review the contracts or terms and conditions you click for privacy or security language. Do those terms sound reasonable? Can you negotiate those terms to ensure your best interests are protected?

- **What do you do now?** Read the company's information security policies or incident response procedures. These documents will set the standard your company will be measured against after an incident, so avoid setting unrealistic expectations or using aspirational language.

- **Create a treasure map.** Understand what kind of data you store and find out who else has access to it. You should conduct an inventory of devices, software, and data to protect them. This is just as essential to a business as keeping a balance sheet.

- **You heard it here first.** Set up Google news alerts for mentions of your company, city, or family. You will find out immediately if Google finds a new mention of you on the internet.[12]

- **Get headline news.** Subscribe to several news feeds or podcasts that talk about security issues. Sources like Brian Krebs are well known for providing insightful investigative journalism in cybersecurity.[13]

- **Find me, follow me.** Follow the companies and individuals you work with on social media—Twitter, LinkedIn, and Facebook—to get real-time updates.

Securing the brain

If you're like most Americans, you spend more than twenty-six minutes commuting to work. Each way. Most commuting experiences fall into one of two categories: bumper-to-bumper with other cars or sitting in an uncomfortable bus or train seat shoulder-to-shoulder with a stranger. If I asked you what happened on your way to work this morning, you probably couldn't remember much, if anything, about the commute. You probably wouldn't remember the makes and models of the cars you drove behind, their license plates, or how much gas you have left in your tank (unless you just filled up).

You might be tempted to just write off this hour every day as the cost of having a job, but there's something important going on inside your mind. It's easy to dismiss your brain as having zoned out, but this isn't the whole picture. You have spent more than two hundred hours in the last year on your commute thinking about work, listening to music, or figuring out what's for dinner. Your brain was able to do two things at once: navigate to your place of business or school and conduct higher-level planning and creative thought.

The purpose of security awareness is to ensure you are free to perform those higher-level functions while navigating the use of technology. When a security expert is interviewed, however, and says we need to have greater security awareness, it sounds a lot like they are scolding people for forgetting about security. At work, the higher-level portion of your brain is checking email, answering phone calls, or listening in meetings or classes. It hasn't forgotten about security; it was simply busy doing work and just missed its exit on the highway.

To understand what's going on, let's look at the exceptions to our zoned-out minds: the cases where you almost got into an accident or were in a confrontation with one of those strangers on the bus. These situations triggered your mind to become fully alert and focused on the present to avoid danger. You got angry. It became personal. And because you got angry, unlike when you were zoned out, you'll be able to recall the colors and movements of every car or person that was around you.

Paul MacLean's 1990 book, *The Triune Brain in Evolution*, introduced the theory of the triune brain.[14] This theory divides the brain into three complexes: the neocortex, the limbic system, and the reptilian brain. The neocortex is the part of the brain responsible for abstract thought, imagination, learning, and planning. The limbic system governs emotions, like fear or anger, and drives, like hunger or caring for offspring. The reptilian brain is the oldest part of the brain and governs instincts and fight-or-flight responses. The theory posits that, as mammals evolved, their brains developed new structures capable of more and more sophisticated reasoning, while less important, repetitive tasks were offloaded to the lower-level complexes. One component of the reptilian brain is the basal ganglia, which neuroscientists have determined is where habits are governed. Your day-to-day email checking, phone answering, and commuting are all delegated to the reptilian complex, so your neocortex is free to focus on higher-level problems.

There are two major differences between the higher-level part of the brain and the lower-level systems: speed and bandwidth. Feelings occur instantly, while rational thought takes time. But feelings have a more limited range. Psychologists Paul Ekman and Wallace V. Friesen studied a tribe in Papua New Guinea called the Fore and found that humans have only six primary emotions: fear, anger, disgust, sadness, surprise, and happiness.[15] The neocortex, in contrast, essentially puts no limit on the range of things it can process.

Your neocortex is allowing you to process the meaning of these words as you read them. But it is your limbic brain that allows you to recognize each word. While you can choose to forget everything you've read thus far, you can't choose not to recognize a word once it is learned and stored in your hippocampus. It is your limbic brain, through the frontal lobe, that makes the decision to keep reading or not.

Understanding these differences in how your brain operates is essential when learning about cybersecurity. These differences explain how you can think about two things at once: driving and planning what's for dinner, or catching up on email and monitoring for phishing red flags. Whether you are preparing your defenses to prevent hackers from getting in, or reacting after something has happened, you will encounter pitfalls along the way because of the way your brain is designed. To overcome these pitfalls, you must be prepared to recognize them.

I went to elementary school in the 1980s. I can still remember the older teachers complaining about how calculators were rotting our brains. We would never be able to do complex multiplication or division in our heads like previous generations, they lamented. I'll never know for sure if using a slide rule would have made me into a mathematician, but the teachers were on to something even if they didn't know it. We have the same complaints today about Millennials and Google or teenagers and smartphones.

Have you ever had a conversation with someone where you can't agree on a certain fact? Where you are both sure of the fact's validity and can produce distinct reasons to support your position? We are now in an age where all the substance of human knowledge is just a few keystrokes away—but rather than bringing us closer to knowledge, it moves us further away. I call this phenomenon the Google block. It's like writer's block, insofar as the brain gets stuck and won't look outside itself for an answer.

To understand why this happens, let's look at how memory works. Our memories are associative, meaning all of the information, ideas, and feelings gathered through past experiences are interconnected. A picture of a mother and daughter may create the emotion of caring in our minds, but it might also make us think of our own mother. Associative memories act as an input to what Nobel Prize-winning psychologist Daniel Kahneman calls System 1, corresponding roughly with the limbic and reptilian parts of the brain. System 1 processes inputs and produces outputs like feelings, impulses, and ideas. Kahneman describes a second system, System 2, corresponding with our neocortex. System 2 communicates with System 1 about what it is seeing (inputs) and how it should respond (outputs).

In his book *Thinking, Fast and Slow*, Kahneman writes, "Brains are lazy."[16] Our minds will always take the information we have at hand and give us the solution requiring the least amount of processing power. The key is that the brain will take information it already has to make an inference. It doesn't ask for more information. The implication is that if we did not have security knowledge before an incident, we are neurologically wired not to consider that we needed it. Kahneman calls this phenomenon "What you see is all there is."

Unfortunately, the story gets even worse. Our brains are wired to have what Kahneman calls cognitive or confirmation bias. Once we decide on something, not only do we fail to look for other information, we actively block out evidence to the contrary. "In terms of its consequences for decisions, the optimistic bias may well be the most significant of the cognitive biases," Kahneman writes.

The phenomenon of "fake news" illustrates this bias. Let's assume you see an inflammatory article on social media. The first thing you may notice is that you're having an emotional response to the story. These types of articles are designed to trigger an immediate response, tricking System 1 into reacting so quickly that System 2 does not have time to reflect. If there were time to reflect, System 2 should ask, "What is the source of the information? Is it a recognized or reputable media outlet? Or a site you've never heard of? If it's a smaller site, look at the About Us page of the site. Who is the editor? Who owns the company? Can you verify this story with multiple media outlets by searching in Google or Bing?"

During the 2016 American presidential election, multiple sources inside Russia created more than three thousand advertisements on the Facebook website.[17] These advertisements were targeted at known swing states, like Florida, where support can drastically change the results of an election. Many of the images the advertisements showed went viral, reaching a dramatically larger audience precisely because of the failure to check sources.

You must have knowledge and experience to make informed decisions. Because of the attention given to fake Facebook ads following the election, it is likely their effectiveness has already been reduced. System 2's job will include generally associating this memory when it comes to security to help trigger the need for checking sources before sharing an inflammatory link or recognizing a link as inflammatory in the first place. To do this effectively, System 2 needs a variety of types and qualities of associated security memories to draw upon.

This variety is also important because each person has a different learning style, and those styles must be considered as you decide on a path for increasing your cybersecurity awareness. Are you a visual learner or more auditory? Do you learn more effectively through experience or through reading? In the next chapter, I'll provide types of exercises for stimulating multiple aspects of your learning style to provide a more effective learning experience.

We don't need to think about security all the time. Instead, we need to have just-in-time security. We must be able to recognize when security issues have come up or are about to come up, and we need to be able to do something about those issues. This process aligns with the definition of literacy. If being literate means recognizing the words on the page, then having cybersecurity literacy means recognizing potential threats. You may need to have experiences to know what to do or how to respond, but maybe you'll just need to Google the answer. The habit of cybersecurity literacy means that you have the foundation necessary for seeking sources to find answers and solve challenges. Now that you've learned to read, however, it's time to stop believing everything that you read.

2

SKEPTICISM

In 1996 the CEO of Texas Instruments, Jerry R. Junkins, died tragically from a heart attack.[1] In the weeks following his passing, there was a fierce political battle for who would succeed him. After the dust settled, Tom Engibous, looking completely exhausted, walked into a small broadcast studio and announced to the company that he would become the new CEO.

The broadcast engineer working with him asked how he was doing, and Engibous responded, "If you are ever in my shoes, promise me you will surround yourself with 'no men' because 'yes men' provide you no value." Engibous would lead Texas Instruments as CEO for eight years and would continue as board chair for another four. The company's stock price increased by five times under Engibous's leadership, more than doubling the average increase in share price for the S&P 500. The broadcast engineer never forgot that advice.

The engineer's name was John Kindervag, and he would go on to create what is now known as the Zero Trust model of cybersecurity, widely recognized as the leading paradigm for securing modern computer networks. But the insight early in his career that you need to challenge the status quo to succeed is what shaped his groundbreaking process. Kindervag's model is based on applying skepticism to cybersecurity network architecture in a more holistic way. Anyone can take the same approach in their own lives, applying skepticism to catchy clickbait headlines or fishy business deals that sound too good to be true.

In the 2000s, the prevailing mindset in computer security was that you needed to focus on securing your perimeter to be cybersecure. This model was so ingrained in the industry that firewall manufacturers labeled the ports on their devices "trust" and "untrust," helpfully telling engineers which connection to plug into the internet and which was okay to connect to the corporate network. You were supposed to trust everything on the inside.

The problem with this model was that when a hacker made it into the network, they had nearly free rein to steal corporate data. The problem, Kindervag observed, is that trust itself is a vulnerability. We misplace our trust when we anthropomorphize a digital system. "We have this idea that it's a person on the network, when in fact it's not," Kindervag said. "People aren't on the network, packets are." A packet is just an electron or photon moving from one place to another that contains some amount of information being exchanged between systems. We shouldn't assign trust to that information based purely on location. Instead, firewalls should be shipped with all ports labeled "untrust."

While this may sound like good advice today, when Kindervag was creating the Zero Trust model as the lead analyst for the research firm Forrester, his idea was ridiculed by other analysts at competing firms. The idea that you needed to be skeptical of your own network and the protections within it turned the model on its head, in part because this went against much of what the cybersecurity vendors were selling at the time.[2]

The support for this approach came instead from practitioners who saw how their networks were being penetrated. With the rise of smartphones, more and more insecure devices were brought into what had been a secure area inside a company. Many employees began working from home and connecting directly into corporate networks, where they could remove data or introduce unexpected vulnerabilities. And with cloud computing, more of the company's servers and services were being moved outside that secure perimeter.

The Zero Trust model offers a flexible alternative: Adopt a least-privilege model, log everything, and secure everything regardless of location.[3]

How does Kindervag incorporate this model into his daily life? Liability and control. He uses credit cards or PayPal instead of cash. Why? Because the liability of any issues falls on those companies. Kindervag uses cloud services for his data rather than setting up his own servers. He's also on Twitter. He can't control his credit card or Social Security numbers from getting lost, but if a service is insecure, he'll avoid it or stop using it altogether. "We apply the word trust to things we can't control," he says. "The idea of trust helps us get through the day and navigate circumstances that we can't control otherwise."

In 1984 President Ronald Reagan met with author Suzanne Massie after reading her book *Land of the Firebird: The Beauty of Old Russia*, in which she chronicled the history of the Russian empire. Massie met with Reagan at least sixteen times during his presidency, an unprecedented level of direct access for a citizen. She would later become an informal messenger between Reagan and Mikhail Gorbachev. When they first met, she taught him an old Russian proverb that translates as "Trust, but verify."[4] This became one of Reagan's most often quoted phrases. He most famously used this phrase in reference to the signing of the 1987 Intermediate-Range Nuclear Forces Treaty with the Soviet Union.

Kindervag says this phrase is meant to be ironic. In Russia, the phrase is a kind of joke. The phrase is meant to imply that you shouldn't have trusted to begin with. Kindervag applies the Zero Trust model to computers, but he doesn't go so far when it comes to people. Should we all be like Fox Mulder from the series *The X-Files* and have posters on our walls that say "Trust No One"? No. But if trust is a vulnerability, then how do we protect ourselves when it comes to human beings? How skeptical do we need to be?

Good judgment

In 1963 Lenore Jacobson read an article in a science magazine that would change her life. The article, written by Harvard psychologist Robert Rosenthal, was about the effect of researchers' expectations on their subjects in psychological experiments.[5] In the article, Rosenthal wondered if a similar notion of self-fulfilling prophecy might be at work in the relationship between teachers and their students. Jacobson, who wore glasses and a big smile, was an elementary school principal at the Spruce School in San Francisco. She wrote to Rosenthal, and together, they agreed to conduct an experiment at her school.

At the beginning of the school year, the students took an IQ test. To test the theory that teachers' expectations have an impact on student outcomes, the researchers told the teachers that some students were superstars with high IQs, while, in actuality, those students had average or below-average intelligence scores. At the end of the school year, the students were tested again, and those below-average students the teachers had been deceived about all showed above-average gains in their IQ.[6]

Similar studies have shown that the reverse is also true. When expectations are low, test scores go down. Rosenthal and Jacobson's experiment illustrated what psychologists call the Pygmalion effect. In Greek mythology, Pygmalion was a sculptor who created a statue of a woman that was so beautiful and realistic that he immediately fell in love with it. He prayed to Aphrodite that she would bring the statue to life, which she did. In effect, Pygmalion's belief became his reality.

There is an unofficial motto in the cybersecurity world: "People are the weakest link." This motto is reinforced by statistics, such as human error accounting for more than 90 percent of all data breaches, according to an IBM study.[7] Recently, I read an article about how people are the one thing that can't be patched. Social engineers, like Kevin Mitnick in his book *The Art of Deception*, like to boast that they are 100 percent successful in breaching companies and always will be.[8] Many people in the cybersecurity industry come from IT backgrounds that familiarize them with acronyms about how users are the problem, like PEBCAK (problem exists between the chair and the keyboard) or ID10T (read as "idiot") errors.

When you look through the lens of the Pygmalion effect at the cybersecurity community's failure to effectively train employees, it starts to make sense why we've been so unsuccessful in changing behaviors. How can we successfully train our employees to be cyber-secure when, fundamentally, we don't believe they are capable of that success? Instead of making positive changes and establishing good discipline around cybersecurity, we are communicating that if we just substitute cynicism for good cybersecurity, then that will be enough. When security professionals train students or employees to be more cybersecure, the training usually boils down to producing a list of things not to do. Don't write down your password. Don't use Facebook. Don't click on links. But the message we are really sending is that to be secure, you need to be cynical. Instead of focusing on good cybersecurity discipline and positive behaviors, we're using cynicism as a shortcut. The result of the cynical approach speaks for itself. It doesn't work.

Skepticism and cynicism can't be synonymous for good security to be possible. Being cynical would mean that we don't believe that we can make a difference. While some may express cynicism, nearly everyone that I've ever worked with believes that they can make a difference. In fact, this belief is what drives them in their careers. We need both skepticism and belief that security is achievable at the same time. We need to feel empowered to trust our judgment.

In his book *The Speed of Trust*, author and management guru Stephen M.R. Covey talks about the idea of a velocity to trust that allows human interaction to work much more efficiently. When trust is missing, there is a tax on relationships that costs both time and money.[9] Covey is the son of Stephen R. Covey, the author of *The 7 Habits of Highly Effective People*. Covey Sr. talks in *7 Habits* about how he delegated care of the lawn to his son. His son learned the valuable lesson that because his father trusted him, he was responsible for whether the lawn was green or brown. Trust, the younger Covey argues, is conveyed through thirteen behaviors that leaders either exhibit, inspiring confidence, or fail to exhibit, using up any remaining goodwill.

If trust reduces friction and increases speed, then skepticism means slowing down. It means taking your time to think carefully about a situation and then asking calculated questions. There is a cost associated with skepticism—it is the tax Covey talks about. To be in proper balance, this cost must always be chosen when considering what is at risk. Asking my Social Security number has a very different value than asking my phone number. This understanding of what is at risk comes from the literacy habit. Literacy means understanding your environment by asking questions without making assumptions.

Part of enabling skepticism means building in the time you need to be skeptical. If you need to pause to spend a few more moments than you would have liked so you can ask more questions, then you should be able to give yourself that space.

When I first began thinking about skepticism, I pictured it like a spectrum with skepticism on one end and trust on the other. What Covey taught me was that skepticism and trust work together like a matrix. You can have both high or low trust and high or low skepticism at the same time. The solution to having what Covey describes as "good judgment" is to have both high trust and high skepticism at the same time.

Listen to your gut

When I became chief information security officer (CISO) at Southern Methodist University, one of the first things I did was bring in a social engineer to walk the campus. In the context of cybersecurity, social engineering is the use of deception to manipulate individuals into divulging confidential or personal information that may be used for fraudulent purposes. Social engineers come into your company and, without knowing anything more than the information a general member of the public would know, try and convince people to let them in and give them stuff they shouldn't be able to get. Sometimes they will walk out with boxes full of files. Other times, they can get access to tamper with sensitive equipment.

As a part of the hiring process, the social engineer requested that we give him a get-out-of-jail-free letter signed by the president of the university, so if he were caught in the act, he could present the letter and, after a few phone calls to verify the letter's authenticity, leave without the police being called. The social engineer assured me that in ten years of doing this work, he had never been challenged or had to present the letter.

Without any preparation, we unleashed him to see what he could find. The university campus is almost a square mile with more than a hundred buildings, so he started by walking through as many as he could get into. On the morning of the first day, I got the phone call. He had been caught. I was stunned and, admittedly, a little bit proud of my university. He hadn't been on campus for more than an hour. We cleared up the issue with the staff who had caught him, and since it was still so early in the engagement, I asked them to keep it quiet so we could continue the assessment. Through the rest of the engagement, no other departments on campus caught him in the act. The group that caught him: our school of theology.

One might think that a school of theology, with some of the most faithful people around, would be more susceptible to social engineering, not less. Skepticism is about questioning, and doubt is a well-established part of the process when you study religion. Rabbi Eric Yoffie, who was head of the largest Jewish denomination in America for sixteen years, argues, "Doubt is the heart of belief."[10] You prepare yourself to answer questions from people having crises of faith or from people new to faith who have doubts that they want to overcome. Thus, those in the school of theology were the only ones who weren't afraid to ask questions about what he was doing.

The real question when it comes to cybersecurity is whether skepticism can be learned. Is it something we can teach employees? Or will they always be doomed to fall for the same old tricks?

In 2014 I began sending my own phishing messages. I wasn't trying to steal passwords or infect computers with malware. Instead, as CISO, I sent them to stop people from clicking on phishing links. I called these simulated phishing campaigns. When a person clicked on one of my simulated messages, they were redirected to a website that had some training about how to recognize phishing messages. The vendor we used to run this service warned us that the first time we did it, we would see click-through rates—that is, the number of people who click on email messages—likely between 40 percent and 50 percent. This number was based on their experience with other organizations our size, and unfortunately, our first campaign saw a 43 percent click-through rate.

Over the next three years, this number fell to only 3 percent, a decrease of about 95 percent. When it comes to the effectiveness of a security control, this was an astounding result. Later, when we saw successful phishing attempts that caused harm, we could look to this number to definitively show a measurable improvement in our security program. What was the secret behind this success story? Was it the vendor we used? Was it the clever phishing messages we used?

It turns out the training wasn't what mattered. We experimented with different vendors and different types of campaigns. The content of the phishing messages wasn't important either—it could be easy or difficult to spot the phish. The frequency wasn't particularly important either. Although I've talked to some CISOs who send simulated campaigns weekly, I only send my campaigns biannually. The effectiveness of this training was based entirely on employees understanding that they could receive a phishing message at any time. They were primed to be skeptical.

When I run into people on campus, they tell me they got my phishing message and they didn't click on it. When I ask further, they tell me all about the phishing message. They don't necessarily know that I only send the phishing messages a couple times per year. But they do realize they need to be on the lookout for phishing messages. I think this helps our community to better understand that the internet isn't a safe place. Instead of learning the hard way, we provide them with a safe method to learn to be skeptical and therefore protected.

Don't pick up the phone

I don't answer my office phone anymore. Because of my role, I usually get around seventy cold calls per week from salespeople looking to introduce me to their company or technology. Usually, they say they just want fifteen minutes of my time. If, somehow, I could accommodate all of these conversations seamlessly into my week, I'd spend about 50 percent of my time talking to salespeople.

Salespeople act a lot like hackers. They use the same social-engineering techniques hackers use, and when they're good at their jobs, they are as good as the most elite social engineers. It's a cool way of thinking about being a salesperson . . . if you're a salesperson. Many roles within an organization require employees to perform research, outreach, and evangelism on behalf of their employers: public affairs professionals, marketing, sales, fundraising, and sometimes human resources. To people outside the organization, these roles can resemble hackers because they set off skepticism alarms. Consequently, an organization can get a reputation for acting like hackers to generate business, creating what Covey describes as a trust tax, as mentioned previously.

In the cybersecurity field, vendors and salespeople can't afford to act like hackers. The security community expects salespeople to be knowledgeable about security. When vendors use social-engineering techniques, it sets off alarm bells in their potential customers' minds. It makes me question whether the person selling security really understands what they're selling. Still, talking to a salesperson is one of the best ways to learn how to combat social engineering.

One of the questions I most frequently receive from salespeople is "Can you tell me who at your company is responsible for x, y, and z?" You can probably get a very good idea of this through LinkedIn, so why would you ask this? If you are a social engineer, you're building a profile of my organization, and you want to get a warm introduction to the target of the attack. So you don't start with the target. You start with someone who has the authority to provide a handoff while avoiding raising any red flags. Since I can't tell the difference between a real salesperson and a hacker impersonating a salesperson, my default is to run with the assumption that you're a hacker until I believe otherwise. Unfortunately, many vendors work hard to prove me right.

Another common type of reconnaissance question both hackers and salespeople use is "What kind of firewalls do you use?" If you are a hacker, and I'm assuming you are, this is helping you profile my network for a future attack or further refine a penetration already in progress.

Another common social-engineering technique is to build authority. Many vendors do this by name-dropping their customers. This isn't a huge problem, and if I see this in a PowerPoint, I'll assume that they've gotten permission from those customers to use their names. But if a vendor does this in passing or to keep me on the phone, it looks like they won't keep their customer's information confidential. If I want a customer reference, I'll generally ask for one. The best salespeople will talk knowledgeably about their experience with other customers in your industry without name-dropping. This protects their existing customers while also sending the message that they will protect your information in the future.

My favorite technique is the guilt-trip email. After doing several cold calls and maybe a few email follow-ups, they'll say, "George, did we do something wrong? This will be our third and final email." If you've gone through any phishing training, no doubt you've seen that a common red flag is setting an artificial deadline to create urgency. With urgency comes emotion, and that emotion can cloud the judgment we need to avoid the trap. This feels the same to me—and it's just a lame thing to say to someone.

Recently, I received a calendar invite from a vendor. Several of my colleagues were included, but not ones I would normally meet with. I had never met this vendor before. I had never exchanged emails with this salesperson. I checked with my colleagues, and none of them had ever had a conversation with this individual either. This technique is similar to many social-engineering tactics; it takes advantage of a natural inclination to just blindly accept meeting invites, particularly when other people have been invited, because you'll assume someone else arranged the meeting and you may not want to look stupid for asking why. Using this sales tactic to get your foot in the door has become all too common, in part because it's highly successful. This technique doesn't seem to be limited to big companies, small companies, startups, or any specific industry.

You need to be on the lookout for these tactics when hackers or social engineers are profiling your environment. They should trigger an internal alarm that you should be skeptical of the motives of the person asking the questions. Be careful not to share details about your organization with people who don't need to know them.

Leaders must listen to the skeptics

On October 1, 1985, Robert Ebeling wrote a memo to NASA that started with one word, "Help!"[11] Ebeling worked for the NASA contractor helping to build the solid rocket motors that propelled the space shuttle into orbit. In the memo, he wrote, "MSFC [NASA's Marshall Space Flight Center in Huntsville, Alabama] is correct in stating that we [his contractor, Morton-Thiokol] do not know how to run a development program." This would be an astonishing criticism by any employee of a company when talking to the company's biggest client. But Ebeling's "Help!" memo became some of the most important pages in the history of NASA. Three months later, after NASA's deputy director, George

Hardy, dismissed Ebeling's concerns, the space shuttle *Challenger* was tragically destroyed, killing all seven people aboard.

Before Thiokol, Ebeling had worked at NASA as a rocket scientist. Since 1977, when the boosters were still being designed, NASA had known that the O-rings they used could fail, resulting in "unacceptable" damage. The problem only got worse as temperatures got colder. Thiokol had only certified the use of the O-rings in temperatures above 40 degrees Fahrenheit. NASA management had largely ignored this advice, despite years of evidence of damage to boosters from failed O-rings. The space shuttle program had been in operation for five years when Ebeling wrote his memo, but rather than stopping all shuttle operations, they decided to continue using the boosters until a new design could be produced.

Instead of slowing down the shuttle program while the problem was being fixed, NASA management wanted to expand the shuttle launch schedule into the winter, which would result in launching under colder conditions. The temperatures for the day of the Challenger launch were predicted to be lower than 20 degrees Fahrenheit. So cold, in fact, that engineers remembered the memo Ebeling had written three months prior. When his manager asked Ebeling what he recommended, Ebeling responded, "We're in no man's land." Ultimately, Ebeling and the other engineers recommended that NASA postpone the launch until the temperatures warmed up in the afternoon. NASA wasn't happy with this advice.

The launch the previous winter was made at 53 degrees and had seen more damage on the booster than any previous launch. Ebeling's suggestion to move the launch to the afternoon was rejected by NASA because the response wasn't based on any hard data, just on his gut instincts. NASA gave Thiokol just two hours to come back with a prepared response. Thiokol had never done a test fire of a rocket in sub-freezing temperatures, so they couldn't provide additional data in that amount of time. Not wanting to lose their biggest customer, the managers at Thiokol agreed to a second conference call without the engineers on the line, and the managers gave in to NASA's pressure and agreed to the launch. Deputy Director Hardy's concern? Having to give up winter launches and wait until April to resume flights. NASA wanted Thiokol to sign a document certifying the launch, but only two out of the three Thiokol managers on the call agreed to sign the document.

The team of engineers at Thiokol all agreed the results of the launch would be catastrophic. As Ebeling drove with his daughter to his office, where they would watch the launch, he told her, "The *Challenger* is going to blow up. Everyone is going to die." Ebeling would blame himself for the rest of his life for not having done more to prevent the tragedy.[12] "I should have done more," he was quoted as saying. But Ebeling had done his job and more, taking a stand when the other engineers at his company and at NASA weren't. What happened to the *Challenger* and the astronauts aboard could have been prevented if NASA had listened to the skeptic.

Ebeling isn't alone.

"The Boy Who Cried Wolf" is one of Aesop's most famous fables.[13] A shepherd boy repeatedly tricks the nearby villagers into thinking a wolf is attacking his flock. The boy is bored, and playing a practical joke is a nice way to pass the time. But when a wolf actually does attack his flock, the villagers ignore his cries. In some versions of the story, the wolf also eats the boy, because no one will come to his aid. The *Challenger* disaster raises a different, opposite question. What if the villagers are so consumed with their own lives that they don't want to hear an honest shepherd's pleas because believing them would be an inconvenience? Human beings tend to ignore good advice every day. They don't wear helmets or seat belts when science says to. People continue to smoke cigarettes despite a printed warning on the label indicating the potential dangers.

The "boy who cried wolf" label is one of the biggest challenges that CISOs face. To avoid being perceived as the boy who cried wolf, they must walk a fine line between making improvements and sounding too many alarms. Many great CISOs have adopted an approach of making themselves partners with the business, helping to build trust and establish credibility so they'll be heard when a breach happens. The difficulty in figuring out how to get someone to listen to bad news isn't limited to security. To get people to listen, you must look at what is motivating those people to act, and then you must provide appropriate incentives.

This mirrors the incentives at work with NASA and Morton-Thiokol. Thiokol wanted to keep the customer happy to mitigate the risk of other contractors successfully bidding on NASA contracts, undercutting Thiokol's service. NASA wanted to put more missions into space and was willing to cut corners with safety to do so.

Another, more recent example of skeptics who predicted a catastrophe involves the 2008 financial crisis. In 2007 Meredith Whitney was the managing director for research at Oppenheimer Holdings, where she performed research on financial markets. That October, she issued a report on the company Citigroup.[14] The report was simple; the company had been paying out more in dividends to investors than it was making in profit. Citigroup's stock fell 97 percent over the next year and a half, and this prediction landed Whitney on the cover of *Forbes* in 2008. She issued report after report that year indicating that the country was on the verge of the biggest financial crisis in history, yet she was attacked for her statements. According to Michael Lewis, author of *The Big Short*, the intention was to discredit her.[15] CEOs of the major banks that began failing or requiring bailouts over the several months following her predictions all made statements that no one could have predicted the collapse. Yet Lewis, in his book, describes several skeptics who were able to successfully predict the collapse of the collateralized debt obligation bubble and turn the disaster into a fortune. How could there be such a huge disconnect between the executives running these giant banks on the one hand and the researchers and analysts predicting their failure on the other?

Susan Cain was an attorney at a Wall Street law firm, representing a bank that was considering buying a portfolio of subprime mortgages. These same subprime mortgages would lead to the 2008 financial crisis. Many of these mortgages had been filed so quickly that the paperwork for the purchase of the homes hadn't been filed properly. When notified about the number of irregularities in the paperwork, Cain noticed the bankers didn't bat an eye. They were unfazed. Cain wanted to know why, and her investigation found that the financial industry was dominated by aggressive, risk-taking executives. Those risk takers were, by and large, extroverts. In her book *Quiet: The Power of Introverts*, Cain writes that introverts and extroverts act differently when taking risks.[16]

Studies suggest that when asked to play different games, extroverts will play aggressively, while introverts will be more cautious. This isn't necessarily surprising, but what happens when the subject loses makes the research interesting. When introverts make a mistake, they slow down and think more about the situation. Instead of slowing down or even staying at the same pace, extroverts speed up. In the words of psychologists John Brebner and Chris Cooper, extroverts are "geared to respond," while introverts are "geared to inspect."[17] If you were an executive at AIG during the 2008 financial crisis, you got there by being "geared to respond," but as Cain describes in her book, this also left you vulnerable to not seeing danger coming. To become a CEO, managers and directors speak up, are seen as outgoing and charming, and make decisions in the face of adversity. The promotion structure, particularly in the financial industry, is one that embraces both risk and extroversion. These are what encourage those same leaders to ignore the advice of the skeptics in the room.

Cain's solution to the dilemma is simple. If you're an extrovert and want to make a gamble or investment, be aware of your propensity to become attracted to risks, and temper those activities by seeking the advice of an introvert who will counterbalance your tendencies. If you're an introvert and you want to engage in a risky activity, like starting a company, talk to an extrovert who can help you seize the right opportunities.

After the *Challenger* disaster, NASA began having what they called "boiler room" discussions. The idea, according to a 2010 memo, was to provide a "forum for healthy debate on the validity of assumptions of 'credibility,' completeness of testing, and applicability of any optional workarounds available to mitigate consequences of failures, should they occur."[18] The changes NASA made also changed the incentive structure at the top. NASA foresaw the very real possibility of ending the shuttle program altogether, and this changed the pressure around launch schedules when it came to safety. Applying this advice to cybersecurity can be overwhelming, but you can begin with something as simple as not ignoring your computer when it tells you to update or patch. Or better still, configure your drive to automatically apply patches. And if your technology person brings forward a potential issue, understand that there may be competing pressures to delay or ignore this issue, and take this as an opportunity to partner with the techie. After all, finding someone willing to go the extra mile is rare, and consequently extremely valuable.

Kindervag, Ebeling, and Cain were all willing to stand up at the right times and be "no men" (and women), and this is one of the reasons they've been so successful in their careers. Still, it's one thing to be skeptical and speak up if the situation calls for it. But when it comes to security, one of the most commonly expressed feelings is that people should be skeptical all the time at the same high level of intensity. I don't share this belief. I think humans should bring the right amount of skepticism with them based on what the situation calls for. This is the habit I call Vigilance.

3

VIGILANCE

Waldo needs your help. Waldo, or Wally, as he is referred to by his friends in the UK, is an unusual guy. You can't miss him. He always wears the same red-and-white-striped shirt everywhere he goes. He even has a matching red-and-white-striped cap. He is always traveling to exotic places and getting lost. Waldo needs you to find him. I'm referring, of course, to the beloved character in Martin Handford's iconic series of books, *Where's Waldo?* The *Where's Waldo?* series has become a worldwide sensation, selling more than fifty million copies and making Handford one of the most successful illustrators of all time.

Handford, like Waldo, is an unusual guy. He has enjoyed drawing since he was a child. From the beginning, though, he was most interested in a specific type of illustration: scenes of crowds. After he graduated from art school, he began working as a freelance illustrator doing what he loved, drawing crowds. He got the idea for an illustrated book full of scenes of crowds, but the publisher had a suggestion. Put a character in the crowds to act as a focal point.[1] This would make people want to look for the character and, consequently, make them study the scenes more closely. Waldo was born.

Some people are born with the magical ability to spot Waldo as soon as they look at the page. He seems to be highlighted, jumping out of the picture. I'm not one of those people. Neither is Randy Olson.

Olson is a computer programmer. Like many computer programmers, he thinks in algorithms and loves to solve problems. So, Olson decided to take up the problem of how to find Waldo most efficiently. As a computer programmer, he called this problem an "optimal search path" challenge. In the words of his blog, he sought to create an algorithm so efficient it would dwarf the experts of the day and "carve a trail of defeated Waldo-searchers in my wake."[2]

To do this, he took in all of the places where Waldo had been to predict where Waldo would be next. There were sixty-eight data points to work with. From a computer perspective, this meant there would be 2.48×10^{96} possible paths between the points, more than all the atoms in the universe. Using just raw number crunching, it would take a supercomputer longer than the universe has existed to solve the problem.

Olson cracked the problem in five minutes using a machine-learning solution called a genetic algorithm. Essentially, a genetic algorithm is a solution that mimics natural selection in order to evolve until the best possible solution is found.

Want to find Waldo fast using Olson's solution? Pick up a Waldo book if you have one or use a Google image search to find one online.

Then you'll need to do two things: filter and scan. The first step requires you to filter out all the extraneous characters in the scene. You can accomplish this by making the okay sign with your hand and looking through the hole made by your thumb and forefinger. Next, you'll need to scan the picture using the optimal path that Olson discovered. The path begins near the bottom left-hand side of the picture. Scan the picture to the right for about two inches, go diagonally up and to the right by four inches, then straight right for another four inches, then down and to the right diagonally by another four inches. The path you'll have traveled will look a little like an upside-down version of the Big Dipper constellation. Based on Olson's data, Waldo is typically found in this search area. Of course, this solution may not be as fun as looking at the crowd for hours and hours, assuming you enjoy that kind of thing.

If you're having trouble finding Waldo, don't worry. The optimal search path isn't designed to find his every appearance. There are a handful of data points that don't fit neatly into that search area. These are called outliers, and they complicate the problem of finding Waldo in a very short amount of time. When you need to find Waldo within a few seconds, you must literally cut a few corners.

Attention to detail

Vigilance involves applying a kind of attention or skepticism toward a given task. When we in the security community give advice like "You should be vigilant at all times," we imply that a normal human is able to be vigilant and perform their everyday tasks at the same time without sacrificing the performance of either. Just like most people aren't born with the natural ability to spot Waldo right off the bat like magic, to be vigilant, you must filter and scan.

Take a phishing message, for example. To effectively protect yourself, you'll need to filter out the extraneous information in your environment: You can't be on a conference call while checking email and expect to be effective at spotting a phishing message, for example. You need to scan for the types of red flags that usually come up in a phishing message. Most security training focuses on learning those red flags but fails to consider the first part of the equation, the filtering, which can make all the difference in effectively identifying those phishing messages or other types of social engineering in the real world.

To be sure, you must be able to spot those phishing red flags, so here are a few tips. Always "hover" or move your mouse over any link in an email or document to make sure that it goes to the intended location. Watch out for even slight differences, like company names being slightly misspelled: "Gooogle" or "Amazoon." Or, even better, use the real Google to search for the site and go directly there instead of clicking a link. If a message was unsolicited or unexpected, you should automatically be more suspicious of its contents. If the message creates a false sense of urgency to encourage you to click, be extra wary of clicking, and use this as a cue to look for additional problems that could confirm the message is a phish. Messages threatening to disable your account if you don't click or telling you your inbox is full are frequently indicators of phishes, as most email providers don't send those kinds of messages anymore. If the message contains obvious spelling or grammatical mistakes, again, use heightened scrutiny, but also be aware that more sophisticated hackers are also using better writers, so this isn't as reliable a red flag as it used to be. Finally, if you just get a gut feeling that the message is suspicious, listen to your gut.

Just like with Olson's search path, there are a few outliers. Not every phishing message has easily identifiable red flags. Several years ago, I heard a story about a conference held for very high-ranking members inside the defense industry, including some multi-star generals. One of the generals received a confirmation message from the conference, and when he clicked on the link, he got a message that the site was busy. A few minutes later, he got another confirmation message, nearly identical to the first, and this time the link worked. He called the conference organizer later and mentioned the site outage. The organizer didn't know what he was talking about because the first message had been a phish. The messages were identical, and he was expecting to receive the email. Even the smartest and most cyber-savvy among us can fall victim if a phishing message is crafted well enough.

Technology can play a big role in preventing phishing. But humans are still the last line of defense, and this defense requires vigilance.

When preparation meets opportunity

It was quiet in Brighton in the early hours of Friday, October 12, 1984, until it wasn't. Brighton sits on the southern shores of England and, because of that, is a popular tourist destination, complete with an amusement park located on the city's only surviving pier. That year, the city was hosting a conference for members of the British Parliament, including Prime Minister Margaret Thatcher. At 2:54 a.m., an explosion rocked the hotel where they were staying. The middle of the hotel collapsed into the basement, leaving a gaping hole in the façade of the building and killing five people, including Sir Anthony Berry, a member of Parliament. The target of the bomb was Prime Minister Thatcher. She and her husband survived.

The bomb had been placed in the hotel nearly a month before by a member of the Irish Republican Army (IRA). The individual had stayed a weekend in the room directly above the suite where Thatcher would stay. He hid the bomb under the bathtub in his room. The bomb was wrapped in clear plastic wrap to avoid detection by bomb-sniffing dogs. It used a videocassette recorder as a long-delay timer. In a chilling message to Thatcher, the IRA said, "We only have to be lucky once—you will have to be lucky always."[3]

Anyone can be lucky once.

When I used to think of vigilance, I pictured a lone soldier in a guard tower, staying up all night waiting for something to happen while he fought off sleep and boredom. In the online, hyper-connected world, this analogy is no longer true. Today, everyone is so busy doing their jobs and keeping up with the pressure to perform that a stealthy attack will almost always slip through. My new definition of vigilance is the state of mind necessary for keeping watch so that when you see something, you can be ready to recognize it and act. It doesn't take any qualifications to win the lottery. But winning the lottery 365 days in a row requires some very specific qualifications: You must have an unfair advantage. The hackers, like the IRA, only have to be lucky once. You need to be lucky year-round.

How does one go about being lucky all the time? You need to be prepared.

The process of being vigilant makes people more prepared. It's like drilling or practice. One of the first things I learned in my cybersecurity career was how to configure firewalls. Configuring a firewall is like telling the post office who will be out of town and shouldn't get mail or who doesn't want to get junk mail anymore. These delivery rules are called policies. One of the things these policies ask you to do after you've said who can get mail and who can't is decide whether you want to create a log of what happened. Logging, as it turns out, is one of the best ways to be prepared for an incident. In the early days of firewalls, storage was extremely expensive, so you didn't necessarily want to turn on logging for fear you might crash the firewall.

The same is true for doors. You might assign keys to an individual, but you don't know who this person will lend their keys to, and maybe they won't always tell you if they lose them. With electronic controls, you can have a detailed audit trail, not just of who has access to a door but of every time they walk through it. When something happens, you can follow a trail of data to figure out what happened. This kind of vigilance helps you learn how to better protect yourself in the future.

Today, the best practice is to log everything and sort out the details in a centralized logging system. These systems are known as security information and event management systems (SIEM). One of the first things hackers learn is how to cover their tracks after they compromise a computer. To combat this, server administrators send their logs off the server that generates them to a central system that stores logs in a forensically secure manner. Rather than just being passive detection systems used for investigations, SIEM tools like Splunk, ArcSight, QRadar, AlienVault, and LogRhythm proactively notify administrators of issues. Splunk even offers free versions for small companies.

Keep that frown upside down

There is a moment in the movie *The Pursuit of Happyness* where Chris Gardner (played by Will Smith) makes a phone call. Or rather, he makes a lot of phone calls. We find out that to make himself more efficient, Gardner never hangs up the phone receiver between calls. He spends six hours each day making phone calls without drinking water to save time going to the bathroom. He must do this because, unlike his younger competitors who have all the time in the world, Chris must pick up his kid from school at a specific time. As we watch him outworking his competition, something amazing happens. We see him smiling. He smiles the whole time he is on the call. In college, I got a similar internship as a financial advisor with a national firm. They had a training program where we learned not just about financial investing but also about basic sales techniques. Making a lot of phone calls is a big part of getting started. To prepare us for this, we were coached, we memorized scripts, and we tried role-playing. The most fundamental advice, however, was to stand up and smile. This advice is hardest to listen to, especially when you're facing so much rejection—I still don't understand how Gardner could smile like that. When you're on the phone, your potential future clients can't read your body language. This limits the emotional connection you can make with them. Standing up and smiling projects your energy through your voice, allows for a more natural conversation style, and puts less pressure on your diaphragm so you can speak more clearly. Even if you're faking a smile, it still works.

This same advice is given today to telemarketers, call center help desks, and receptionists everywhere. I'm here to tell you frowning also comes with benefits—and I use a mnemonic that can help change the way we teach people to be more cybersecure. I call this technique "Slow down and frown."

When a person smiles, it releases endorphins and serotonin into their body, which, in turn, results in relaxation. In 1988 psychologist Fritz Strack ran a famous study that asked ninety-two students to read cartoons taken from Gary Larson's *The Far Side*.[4] The participants were first asked to read the comics while holding a pen in their nondominant hand, then in their teeth (which simulated a smile), and finally with just their lips (which simulated a frown). The subjects reading a cartoon while holding the pen between their teeth to simulate a smile perceived the cartoon as funnier than the baseline of just holding the pen in their hand. Strack believed that smiling tricked the brain into releasing endorphins because the person felt safe. When the subjects frowned, however, they found the comics less funny than holding the pen in their hand. The brain doesn't distinguish between happiness and safety or sadness and vulnerability. Psychologists believe frowning sends a signal to the amygdala, a small part of the brain, indicating that the environment has become unsafe (emotionally or physically) and individuals should exhibit increased vigilance.[5] Researchers have also found that vigilance increases when a person is sad, or even just pretending to be sad.

In a study designed to help protect cyclists, researchers in the UK had drivers watch a short video. They were asked to count how many times one of two teams passed a basketball. At the end of the video, every subject guessed correctly: thirteen. This was a simple activity their minds could easily accomplish. The subjects were then asked, "Did you notice the moonwalking bear?"[6] When the researchers reversed the video, the subjects were shocked to see a man in a bear costume performing breakdancing moves while the basketball teams moved around him. The bear is like the cyclist on the road before a distracted driver, or in cybersecurity terms, the phishing email red flag that gets lost because you're focusing on other tasks.

To combat this, I suggest using the slow-down-and-frown technique. With this method, you keep a frown on your face as you focus on scanning email for threats. This technique will help you be vigilant.

When we train people about phishing, we show them the red flags to look for. Knowing what those red flags are and spotting them are two different things. What's missing is active engagement in looking for those red flags. When someone's mind is engaged in a different activity, like reading the content of the message or thinking about a response, their ability to successfully identify a red flag is diminished, sometimes almost to zero. Using the slow-down-and-frown technique naturally boosts your vigilance level while limiting your focus to just the activity of scanning for threats. With practice, this process can make you more productive.

Reducing distraction is another technique that can also dramatically increase focus. In his book *Deep Work*, Cal Newport describes a 2008 study at the University of Michigan in which subjects were given a complex task to accomplish.[7] Before starting the task, one group of subjects had to navigate a busy downtown city environment, dodging cars and other pedestrians. The second group was sent on a walk on a quiet nature trail where they could let their subconscious consider the problem without distractions. The group who took the nature walk, which gave them time to focus, outperformed the distracted city walkers by up to 20 percent. Eliminating distractions in your office not only increases your productivity, as Newport argues, but can also help make you more secure.

I recommend combining Newport's advice with the slow-down-and-frown technique to help increase your productivity while becoming more secure. This combination requires one simple change in how you use email. Separate the tasks of reading email and responding to email. By focusing solely on reading email, you will boost your skepticism. You will also better prioritize your work and eliminate informational messages, all while helping to reduce distractions. While you read your email, frown. When responding to a message, you can start smiling again . . . if you want.

Avoid creating an environment where completing normal tasks is given a false sense of urgency. Take, as an example, a CEO who demands everything be given to him immediately and without question. When a human resources employee receives an urgent email demanding the whole payroll list from a CEO like this, they will abandon all vigilance and respond immediately without working through their normal vetting process for sharing sensitive information.

This scenario describes CEO fraud. The FBI estimated CEO fraud cost businesses more than $2 billion in 2016.[8] This could be a business-ending scenario for most small businesses. If we simply slow down and use our frown, there might be a lot less fraud. You'll be smiling later.

Timing is everything

When I was in college, I worked with a direct marketing firm as a summer job. This is a fancy way of saying I stuffed envelopes, professionally. We would spend the whole week stuffing envelopes, but we would wait to mail them all at once rather than putting them in the mail as we finished each one. Thursdays were mail days. This was because the company had done the research to find that people are more likely to read their mail when they receive it on the weekend than if they get it on a weeknight after being at work all day. The marketers were smart: They sent their mail on a particular day to maximize the effect their campaigns would have.

The people that send you phishing messages do the same thing. And in 2018, the number of phishing attempts doubled. When an individual gives their password away to a phisher, we've seen hackers read email and even forward all email to a burner address where they can continue to get email even after a user changes their password. And if they've reused that password, other accounts associated with that person could also be compromised.

One of the most sophisticated phishing campaigns that I've seen happened in March 2015 on a snow day when all of Dallas was essentially shut down. While we caught the campaign quickly, it presented more of a challenge given that many administrators were out. Experts suggest that phishers are more likely to send phishing messages in the late afternoon when users are more vulnerable. The explanations for this include that users are simply tired, distracted, or stressed out, or that hackers are perhaps located in different time zones.

To better protect ourselves, we need to understand that we are more vulnerable in the afternoon and why.

In his book *When: The Scientific Secrets of Perfect Timing*, author Daniel Pink argues that *when* you do something is perhaps more important than people think. "Our cognitive abilities do not remain static over the course of a day," he argues.[9] One study by neuroscientist and chronobiologist Russell Foster suggests that the difference in performance between the best part of the day and the worst is the equivalent of consuming the legal limit of alcohol.[10] In study after study of children in schools, the time of day difference accounts for 20 percent of the variance in performance on tests. But this isn't the end of the story. Another study by psychologist Simon Folkard found that the best time to perform a specific task can depend on the nature of that task.[11] And tasks that require vigilance have a specific time of day in which you can expect peak performance: the morning. There is also a specific time of day in which you can expect the worst performance: the middle of the afternoon.

Researchers at Duke University were looking at the effects of harmful errors when giving patients anesthesia. They looked at ninety thousand surgeries across multiple hospitals and found that harmful errors are three times more likely for procedures that begin at 3:00 p.m. as compared to those in the morning. Another study suggests that if you have to have a colonoscopy, you should also do it in the morning. When looking at actual results from across the country, doctors found about half as many polyps in the afternoon, though statistically speaking it should have been an equal number. Other studies looking at handwashing found that surgeons are less likely to wash their hands in the afternoons, increasing rates of infection in patients for surgeries in the afternoon.

I wondered if Pink's theory was also true when it came to cybersecurity.

Many companies today send simulated phishing messages to their employees. As I've mentioned, I've used this technique quite a bit as well.

Over the past five years, I've sent more than twenty thousand phishing messages to students, faculty, staff, and contractors. For those who actually clicked on the link in the phishing message, it was, on average, eight times more likely that they would click on the link in the afternoon rather than the morning. This was true no matter what tool we used to send the phishing messages or how challenging it was to detect them. Phishing messages were always more successful in the afternoons with clicks spiking between 3:00 p.m. and 5:00 p.m.

There was an even more unexpected correlation of this effect as well. When we experience any phishing at the university, users call the help desk to report it. The rate of users tracking their help desk tickets goes up by nearly double in the mornings, when users are able to be more analytical. And the reporting effect isn't limited to just when we run simulated phishing campaigns; users have been more than twice as likely to report phishing in the morning for the past two years.

This has significant implications for how organizations should conduct simulated phishing exercises in the future. Many CISOs I've spoken with complain about how they often reach a plateau in the percentage of users who click on simulated phishes. Limiting our campaigns to the afternoons when we are most vulnerable will have a higher impact than conducting campaigns throughout the day from 8:00 a.m. to 5:00 p.m. or around the clock.

Sharing this book with your boss probably isn't likely to result in your getting the afternoon off. But knowing that your vulnerability to phishing or social engineering increases in the afternoon can help you to be prepared and therefore more vigilant. As Pink suggests, you can adjust your schedule to prioritize analytic activities, like checking email, during the morning and move creative activities like meetings or presentations to the afternoon.

This kind of phishing training is extremely valuable, but employees need to be prepared to receive the training. If it catches them by surprise, this can create an adversarial relationship between the employee and a company, which should be avoided. We send an email explaining the program about two weeks before the campaign begins so that expectations about what to do are set should an employee click on the simulated email: how to report it, what will happen if they click, and so on. The employee needs to feel like they are part of the security team and can be proactive, which is why many security programs also have a phishing reporting mailbox.

A number of companies, such as Proofpoint, MediaPRO, Mimecast, or KnowBe4, provide simulated phishing services, and an open-source software project called Gophish provides the software to run your own simulated phishing service for free. For small companies, you can also just send simulated phishing messages from your own email service with a link to a webpage explaining the training.

The threat center of the brain

During the American Revolutionary War, one of the earliest British victories came when they defeated the American forces and took Bunker Hill, one of the unoccupied hills surrounding Boston. In turn, this led to British control of Boston Harbor. The well-trained and well-equipped British forces didn't expect much of a fight from a poorly organized militia. The British took heavy losses in the battle and only won after the colonists ran out of ammunition and retreated. Knowing they had limited supplies, the leaders of the colonial troops sent the command, "Don't fire until you see the whites of their eyes."

This is an extraordinarily personal command. When you can see someone close enough to see the whites of their eyes, you begin to understand what they're thinking, how they feel. Just by seeing the whites of a person's eyes, you can tell if they're happy, angry, or surprised. Your own brain responds involuntarily to the mental state of the other person. Examine the two pictures below. Each is just a black background with only a glob of white, but you'll immediately recognize that these images are the whites of a person's eyes with the rest of the picture blacked out.

On the left, the whites of the individual's eyes express fear. On the right, the individual's eyes express happiness. When you looked at the image on the left, before you were even able to recognize what the picture was, your heart rate increased. In addition to its role in sadness referred to earlier, the human response to fear is believed to be controlled by the amygdala, which taps directly into a superfast neural channel in the brain that processes emotions. Researchers placed subjects into a brain scanner and showed them the pictures above for less than 2/100ths of a second, not long enough for them to register having seen the image.[12] This superfast neural channel bypasses the visual cortex, saving precious seconds so the human can react to a threat even before they are fully conscious of it. The colonists' rallying cry to shoot when you see the whites of their eyes would have given the revolutionary forces an instinctual advantage.

Unlike in the Revolutionary War, hacking doesn't happen face-to-face, and people can't see their hacker's eyes. On the battlefield, the hundredths of a second can mean life and death. In cybersecurity, you can take as long as you need to read an email or decide to click on a link. The brain didn't evolve to protect itself from threats online, and different strengths are required. We don't need further strengthening of the amygdala; we need better concentration, attention, and awareness regarding threats and vigilance. The surprising answer? Meditation.

In 2013 a team of neuroscientists at the University of Pittsburgh and Carnegie Mellon University conducted several MRI scans on patients both before and after an eight-week course on mindfulness meditation.[13] The scans showed that after the patients had mediated, the amygdala appeared to shrink. As the amygdala shrank, the brain's prefrontal cortex became thicker. The prefrontal cortex is associated with higher-level brain functions like awareness, concentration, and decision-making. The connectivity between the amygdala and the rest of the brain also changed, so that while connections with the amygdala got weaker, connections in the brain associated with attention and concentration got stronger. In other words, all of the areas of the brain that play a role in vigilance got stronger after regular meditation.

The face of the enemy

Jordan Mauriello was standing in what looked like a miniature version of NASA's mission control center. Several large screens dominated the front wall of the security operations center (SOC). Behind the main screen were rows and rows of workstations where security engineers performed analysis of logs and work investigations for customers around the world. The big screens were for the customers who wanted tours of the SOC—just for show. The real magic happened at the analyst workstations. For weeks, Mauriello's analysts had been seeing indicators of compromise (IOCs) related to a new version of cryptojacking malware affecting several of their clients. While ransomware shuts down a computer until you pay a ransom, cryptojacking malware silently steals a computer's CPU cycles to mine Bitcoin, filling the hackers' pockets without the company knowing anything is wrong. Mauriello could hear the frustration in his analysts' voices when they said, "Ugh, there it is again," before beginning the cleanup process again. Something about this malware was different. It was cleverly evading the most advanced antivirus software deployed by Mauriello's clients.

Mauriello has worked in cybersecurity for nearly twenty years and looks more like a character out of *Mad Men* than the stereotype of a gray-bearded computer wizard. He started his career in cybersecurity in the US Navy, where he learned the basics of cryptography, encryption, and forensics. "There was no US Cyber Command when I started," recalls Mauriello. Cybersecurity skills were all developed on a volunteer basis when calls to sign up for courses went out to enlisted guys. For Mauriello, this led to more and more opportunities, which eventually led him to deployments in Iraq for Operation Enduring/ Iraqi Freedom and Joint Task Force Liberia in 2003. Eventually, he ended up in a room doing presentations to the Joint Chiefs of Staff.

Mauriello kept putting his hand up and is now the senior vice president of managed services for Critical Start, a cybersecurity company based in Dallas. Before Critical Start, Mauriello managed the global SOC for Experian, where he faced off against hackers employed by large governments and organized crime syndicates looking to steal financial information.

In the military, guards stationed stateside in watch positions have issues maintaining their vigilance. These soldiers are sometimes dismissed as "untrainable," says Mauriello. But when the same soldiers go overseas and are stationed near the enemy, the reality of an opposing force awakens them. They become extraordinarily vigilant. When they come back home and try to impart their new mindset on their fellow soldiers, it's like looking into a mirror. They have the same challenge their leaders had with them just a few months or years prior. If your enemy is nameless and faceless, if there's nothing that you can do to repel or stop them, engagement goes down. But when the enemy has a very real presence, when you can act against them, it's different. It's like you can see the finish line at the end of a race, and you begin to quicken your pace as though you're running downhill. In Mauriello's words, "You'd be surprised at how suddenly engaged analysts become."

The cryptojacking software Mauriello's analysts in the SOC were seeing ran AutoIt, an automated scripting engine that was originally released in 1999. It is an independent, self-contained binary interpreter that doesn't use any of the interpretive scripting engines native to the operating system. As a binary, AutoIt isn't malicious; all it does is interpret the scripts before processing and running them. Modern antivirus companies know about malicious scripts and will prevent them from running in common interpreters like PowerShell, but when Mauriello's team first discovered the attack, this wasn't true of AutoIt scripts.

Everything changed when an analyst said, "Hey, I think this is the same guy." The analyst had factored the scripts and realized several IOCs could all be attributed to a single actor. All of a sudden, the team was 100 percent engaged. They wanted to find out where the attack was coming from, what it was, how he was doing it, and how he was updating it. Several events coming into the SOC independently didn't create much interest. But when the team finally started putting those events together, it generated a lot of excitement because the team was able to create a campaign to stop the bad guy. They wanted to write a blog article about how they found the attack.

In Mauriello's words, "Everything we do in the SOC should have an impact." To keep the analysts in the SOC vigilant, they have to believe what they're doing will impact the attacker by disrupting his attacks, frustrating or distracting him, or tracing him back to a location where they can notify law enforcement to intervene. Vigilance becomes easy when the attacker has a face or a name.

Fat Panda, Fancy Bear, ILOVEYOU, Blaster, Heartbleed, and WannaCry—if all these words sound a little ominous, that's because they are the names of the bad guys in the Wild Wild West of the internet. Every computer virus gets its own name. Today, the name is usually given to it by the researcher who first finds and discloses the virus. Sometimes hackers even embed their own code names into the viruses they write for researchers to find. Cybercriminals also have names: APT1, Anonymous, or LulzSec. Sometimes, malware or cybercriminals even get their own logos. Why do we give these groups names instead of just assigning numbers to each bit of malware? Because we want to put a face to the faceless enemy. We want to put a name to the nameless. To successfully maintain our own vigilance, hackers can't be the faceless guy in a dark room wearing a hoodie.

One of the first questions leaders ask during an incident is "Who is this attack coming from?" Often, cybersecurity practitioners don't have the answer to that question. On my own team, it's tempting to respond to my executives or our board by saying we just don't have the resources to know the answer. Our team isn't big enough to spend time tracking down all of the bad actors focused on exploiting the specific weaknesses in higher education versus those targeting the retail or banking industries. In Mauriello's experience, when he was able to put a face to the group that was attempting to break into his systems, when he was able to tell the story of why that group was attempting to break in and how he figured out what they wanted to do with that information, the company's leadership tripled his security budget.

Not everyone has the option of tripling their security budget. But whether you have an unlimited budget or no funding at all, the most common path that everyone takes is to start with what matters most to you or to your organization. I call this habit Secrecy.

4

SECRECY

One year, I asked for a video game for Christmas. This was back when video games still had cartridges and came in a package about the size of a book. So, when I saw this familiar shape with some Santa Claus wrapping paper around it, I knew I had gotten what I wanted. I usually had two hours after school where I would be by myself before my parents got home. And I really wanted to play this new video game. One day, I couldn't stand the wait and I unwrapped the game. Instead of playing it right away, I took out the cartridge and closed the box back up, then proceeded to rewrap the gift. I followed all the folds in the paper to wrap it exactly like it had been before, but, unfortunately, as careful as I had been, I tore some paper when I pulled away the clear scotch tape. I went into the hallway closet and found the same wrapping paper, and using the other wrapping as a template, I rewrapped the video game exactly as it had been. I went on to play that video game for several weeks before Christmas. My parents never connected the dots to the video game that I'd be playing on the TV to the one under the tree. I've since admitted this to them, and their response was one of both astonishment and lack of surprise—probably better described as disappointment.

Looking back, I can say I learned several things from this experience. First, in hindsight, this was a fantastic way for me to learn how to wrap gifts. Second, I will definitely know the signals and tricks to look for when my kids have presents under the tree. Employing all those tricks will be part of the fun for me. Third, and most important, I think this was how I first really began to understand the application of the habit of secrecy in a concrete way.

Secrecy is the natural barrier between what is public and what should be private. This barrier is a healthy part of every human experience and is so integral to our function in society that it is a guaranteed protection in the Fourth Amendment of the US Constitution's Bill of Rights. But with secrecy comes a delicate balancing act: Where that barrier falls can change depending on what the secret is. The government might classify one piece of information as top secret, while another piece might only be confidential and others might be public. This approach has the benefit of focusing your protections on the highest levels of secrecy while also allowing individuals inside the organization to freely communicate about less secret information, facilitating collaboration and increasing productivity.

But contracts and other protections alone won't guarantee that your secrets stay secret. If you have something people think is particularly valuable, you should expect that they will try and steal it.

Corporate espionage is just as real as a kid unwrapping his Christmas presents early. In 2000 Microsoft was embroiled in an antitrust lawsuit with the Justice Department over its bundling of the Internet Explorer web browser.[1] At stake was the breakup of Microsoft, perceived as a monopoly, by the US government, due in part to practices the trial judge in the case ruled as predatory. The DC Circuit Court of Appeals later accused the judge of ethics violations for conducting media interviews during the trial.

At the time, an unusual thing was happening in and around the DC-area law and lobbying firms representing Microsoft. At the head of those activities was one of Microsoft's biggest rivals, Oracle. At one firm, a man walked in asking for directions and stole two laptops. At another, several people tried to get into the building but failed. At another, private detectives bribed their way into getting to a company's trash.[2] Larry Ellison, Oracle's founder, stepped forward in 2000 and admitted he had hired the detective. The goal was to find dirt to help disband Microsoft and open the door for Oracle to step in.

Oracle was a corporate competitor attempting to steal dirt on Microsoft. But it wasn't the only, or even the most well-funded, organization to go after Microsoft. Some governments wanted Microsoft's code. In 2004 it was reported that the company's Windows 2000 and Windows NT source code had been leaked and portions of it were circulating on the internet. According to leaked US diplomatic cables from 2009, posted to WikiLeaks in 2010, the Chinese government reportedly hired the same hackers that created the Blaster worm and, using stolen Microsoft code, infiltrated Google and plotted cyberwarfare against US government sites.[3]

Several kinds of groups conduct hacking activities; they vary in sophistication, funding, and capabilities. Organized crime groups have significant funding and can exploit vulnerabilities in networks, usually with a financial goal in mind. Organized crime groups want to extort victims with ransomware, install cryptomining software, obtain access to credit card or Social Security numbers, or attempt to transfer funds directly out of an institution via fraudulent invoices or diverting direct deposits. Nation-states may target research information or intellectual property, but their reach and capabilities are nearly limitless. In 2017 the NotPetya virus was launched by Russia. It targeted computers in Ukraine, but the damage didn't end there.[4] The blowback from the Russian cyberweapon reportedly caused an additional $10 billion in damages to companies around the world, just accidentally.[5] And "hacktivists"—those with social or political motivations for hacking computer systems—may target organizations because of their affiliations or because they are connected to controversial topics. So, how can you protect yourself? The first step is classifying your data.

Classify your data

Thomas was twelve years old when he was kicked out of school. It wasn't that he wasn't smart enough or that he didn't do any work. His teachers were frustrated with his constant questions. They said he'd never make it. In a way, the teachers were right about him: Thomas never went to college. He had trouble holding jobs because of the pranks he played or because the experiments he conducted blew up or started fires. But what others saw as his greatest weakness turned out to be his greatest strength. Thomas was curious.

Thomas's mother began homeschooling him. With her encouragement, he built a lab in his room to conduct the same experiments he saw in famous magazines. When he got a job, he began to take things apart and put them back together again to see how they worked. When he was fired, which happened frequently, he bounced back in large part because he could fix things when they were broken. He also learned how to improve things. He became an inventor. Thomas sold his first invention when he was twenty-four.[6] He went on to receive more patents than any other single person in history. Thomas Edison has been a household name across the world for more than a hundred years.

What is the difference between the stories of Thomas Edison and Johann Gutenberg? As discussed in the introduction, Gutenberg made a lot of mistakes. Gutenberg didn't consult with an attorney when drafting his partnership agreement. He trusted the wrong people. But Edison's and Gutenberg's stories diverge in other key ways.

One of the biggest differences between Edison and Gutenberg was their ability to innovate, and this innovation was made possible because of secrecy. Gutenberg's press company failed after Gutenberg's departure because it stopped innovating. Johann Fust and Peter Schoeffer, the men who took over Gutenberg's press, didn't anticipate the intense competition that would happen after the printing press became a commercial success. Other inventors were able to keep up and continue innovating, quickly surpassing the original design. Edison, in contrast, continued to outpace his competition.

How did he do this?

Edison had serious competition. Like Google or Facebook today, Edison was getting a lot of attention. His "invention factory" in Menlo Park, New Jersey, was so famous that tourists came to walk down the first street in the country to be lit by electric lights at night. Competitors would see one of Edison's inventions and immediately begin offering their own products. Edison saw this and quickly invested more research money into improving beyond his competition and beating them to market with his ideas.

Competitors would have felt intense pressure to infiltrate Edison's young company and steal his secrets. His company was growing quickly. While he may have been able to start his company with a handful of engineers he trusted, he couldn't have vetted every new employee. Up to this point, Edison had personally contributed to every project and knew every employee. As the number of employees increased, he had to divide the work. He chose to divide the research and development efforts into projects. This allowed employees to focus directly on tasks and have ownership of the outcomes, but it also limited access to information to that group. Dividing the work into different projects also meant that no one employee, other than Edison, had visibility into all of the projects. Early on, Edison's project notes were kept on scraps of paper and thrown haphazardly into drawers. Then he introduced lab-specific notebooks, and different projects kept experimental data separate from one another.[7] Essentially, Edison built a firewall between his projects by altering the structure of his organization to prevent his secrets from being leaked.

Had all this work been conducted haphazardly, with no accounting or logs, hiding fraud would have been easy. But the culture of tracking data sent a signal to the employees that fraud would be discovered. At the same time, the importance of the data sent the message that it should be protected. Accountants kept detailed records of the hours spent working on each project and the materials costs. Edison hired a single individual to keep track of the daily work conducted in the labs, which was compiled and sent to Edison. Since he personally reviewed the activity logs, everyone knew malicious activity would be detected.

Edison's approach to keeping secrets was far ahead of its time, but it had one weakness. It made Edison, and Edison alone, the keeper of all secrets. This worked for him when his company was small. How would you protect a global corporation or even a government that employs thousands of individuals and contractors?

If we met in person and I asked you to tell me your deepest, darkest, most embarrassing secret, you probably wouldn't. Knowing what that secret was in your own mind probably took no time at all. How do you know when to keep a secret and when to be open? This process happens instantly for an individual. The memories of those secrets aren't being processed by the slow neocortex. Instead, secrets are protected at a deeper, faster level. And protecting those secrets when they're a part of you becomes automatic. But protecting your company's secrets isn't as straightforward because you need to coordinate with others to keep them. How does everyone know what should be kept secret and what can be talked about openly? How do you know who is authorized to know some information and who isn't? One person might need to know a lot of information to do their job, but they don't need access to everything all the time.

You may have watched spy movies where someone says, "This information is need to know." Usually, a dramatic power struggle between the spy and his handler ensues, the spy always arguing that it is a matter of life and death that they must know the information. All Hollywood scripts aside, the question is simple: Do you need to know this information to do your job right now? It eliminates gossip. Collectively, this concept is known in the security community as "least privilege."

The owner of the data determines who should access it. Least privilege solves the Hollywood problem of whether someone needs to know something by classifying data into several buckets: public, private, secret, top secret, and so on. The "who" that has access is sometimes defined as someone in a certain job or role, in which case this is referred to as role-based access. When the "who" is defined on a case-by-case basis as people request access, it is referred to as discretionary-based access, since access is at the discretion of the data owner.

Just like the government separates its data into several classification buckets, individuals and businesses must also have this kind of classification to properly protect data. Different kinds of controls can be put in place to appropriately protect information based on its classification level. As you move on the spectrum from information that is widely known (public) to information that could cause harm, embarrassment, or loss (secret), more and more controls may become necessary or appropriate. For example, public information may appear freely on a company website, but the secret formula critical to the success of your company may be encrypted and password protected.

Data classification also serves to remind the individual accessing the information about how the information should be handled. While some cases of individuals mishandling information exist, these cases of misconduct can be addressed through proper accounting of access to information and auditing.

Implement effective controls

Steve Jobs and Bill Gates walk into a meeting. No, it's not the beginning of a nerdy computer joke. It is more of a legend, really. By 1983 Apple had released an early version of its Apple Lisa operating system, and Jobs wanted Microsoft to be Apple's first third-party software developer. Apple had a breakthrough product that was a year away from being released, something that would change computers forever—the mouse. The computer mouse had been invented in the 1960s, but it was expensive. This limited use to university campuses and computer research labs. Apple had figured out how to make them cheap and compatible with its new desktop interface. But this wasn't enough. Jobs needed Gates to write software that would let people do stuff with the mouse. He also needed Gates to keep this a secret until after the launch. In November 1983, Jobs's fear came true when Microsoft announced a new computer operating system called Windows that would let users use a mouse.[8]

Gates was called into Apple, and Jobs went crazy. Jobs is said to have screamed, "I trusted you, and now you're stealing from us!"

In his biography on Jobs, Walter Isaacson writes that Gates calmly responded, "Well, Steve, I think there's more than one way of looking at it. I think it's more like we both had this rich neighbor named Xerox, and I broke into his house to steal the TV set and found out that you had already stolen it."[9]

This image of two of the biggest business icons in computer history arguing over the future of computing captures the essence of what secrets are and how important it is to protect them. Both Gates and Jobs are good examples of how businesses approach their secrets. Apple didn't invent the computer mouse. Apple didn't invent the graphical user interface. Jobs improved on both and tried to protect his secrets in his contract with Gates. Jobs had made one error in the contract; it only required Gates to keep the secret for two years—to provide enough time for Apple to release its visionary software. When Apple hit delays, this created a window for Gates to beat Jobs to the punch. From the beginning, Apple kept its secrets close to the vest. Even to this day, Apple keeps its new product and software releases secret until the special events planned months or years in advance. Apple has been known to fire employees who even accidentally leak product details early, as was the case with a developer who accidentally left a new version of the iPhone at a bar, where it was given to a journalist who leaked details online.[10]

When it came to auditing his employees, Gates was a master. Gates recently admitted that, even as early as 1970, he memorized his employees' license plates to know who was coming into the office early or staying late.[11] Gates started Microsoft away from larger cities, which is one way he chose to protect his secrets. He chose Redmond, Washington, where he already lived, rather than relocating to Silicon

Valley. He also became known for pioneering the Silicon Valley practice of giving low salaries and offering big stock options, giving employees a stake in what they were working on, which took away any incentives his employees might have for divulging information to his competitors.

Jobs and Gates approached keeping their company secrets in different ways. Jobs protected his secrets with a contract, but when his contractual protections ran out, he was vulnerable. Gates used silence to protect his secrets. He worked on his project internally and didn't involve outsiders until he made his announcement. He traded the knowledge of his secret for the marketing buzz it would generate. But there's a third person in this story: Alan Kay. Xerox, Alan Kay's employer, took an entirely different approach. The company decided to just give its secrets away, hoping to license them.

Kay is one of the fathers of object-oriented computer programming. He was also the creator of the modern graphical user interface (GUI).[12] These were just the beginning. Kay really wanted to invent a tablet so simple even a child could use it. This was 1968. Human beings hadn't yet landed on the moon. Phones were still the size of a pumpkin. Even the television show *Star Trek*, which débuted in 1966, hadn't thought of something so audacious. The closest thing the visionary television series had was the tricorder, which was just a smaller, more versatile Geiger counter with a calculator built in. Kay didn't just want to dream up the tablet; he expected to build it. At Xerox. In 1970—thirty years before the first computer tablet and a decade before even the first bulky personal computers would hit the market. The innovations of object-oriented computer programs, GUIs, and the computer mouse were all just stepping-stones to this dream. Kay called this device the Dynabook.

Xerox couldn't pull off a device like the Dynabook with 1970s-era technology. Xerox was famous for another, entirely different product— the copy machine. Copiers were an intensely lucrative business, and Xerox was so synonymous with this technology that people used the term "Xerox" instead of "making a copy" (e.g., "I'm going to Xerox some materials for you" or "Get me ten Xeroxes for the meeting"). Kay was a researcher, pushing the leading edge of computing, but the executives at Xerox, unlike those at Apple or Microsoft, weren't interested in creating a computer revolution. So, instead of keeping their secrets secret and letting that research die in some dark closet somewhere, Xerox decided to do something different. They decided to share. They invited people like Jobs and Gates to their Palo Alto Research Center (PARC) and showed off the technology. Xerox couldn't pull off the Dynabook themselves, but they could license the technology and sow the seeds that would lead to it.

Looking at Edison again, one of the first controls he used was isolation. Edison was twenty-nine when he bought thirty-four acres of land in a rural area of New Jersey where a planned housing development had failed just a few years earlier. This remote location served as a secret lab for building and improving upon his inventions. Imagine what the Menlo Park lab must have looked like from the outside. The mostly rural community around those five warehouses would have seen bright, dazzling lights peeking from the doors and windows all throughout the night, not the flickering of candles or lanterns that people were used to. The local paper began referring to Edison as a "wizard."[13] Eventually, Edison had two hundred employees, and the community around them would have been invested in protecting those jobs by reporting suspicious activity. This would have formed another protective layer like a trip wire around Edison's isolation strategy.

Jobs, Gates, Kay, and Edison were all using different kinds of controls. The purpose of these controls was to maintain the right level of secrecy for the company and the type of information they were trying to protect. A security control can be any safeguard or countermeasure that helps an individual or organization prevent, detect, or mitigate risks to its information.

What does an effective control look like? First, you need to know the answers to several other questions. You need to know what it is that you're protecting. In Chapter 1, we discussed creating an inventory of all of the things you're trying to protect. Then, as discussed previously, those things must be classified. Your classification should also consider any compliance, regulatory, or contractual requirements to protect the data. You will also need to identify the threats to your data or systems. Are you protecting yourself from organized crime or from nation-state attackers? How might those actors attempt to get in? The goal of this book isn't to provide an exhaustive list of all of the different kinds of security controls available to you but to help you understand the process of finding the answers. There isn't a one-size-fits-all solution to cybersecurity controls. Churches are different from corporations and will need different types of controls. Families are different from governments and must consider different types of protections. That brings us to the next questions to ask: Once I have all of the information classified and I know what the threats are, what's next? Is there a methodology?

There is a Chinese proverb that says, "The best time to plant a tree was twenty years ago. The second-best time is right now." The same is true of your security controls. Hopefully, you already have controls in place. If not, now is a good time to start. Just like trees, controls have a lifespan, and at what point you select a control determines the methodology you must use to select the right control.

You need to consider controls at the beginning, in the middle, and at the end of a project or service. If you are starting a project or creating a new service, you can look at best practices or what other people are doing to protect themselves. In contracts, lawyers refer to this as "industry standards." After the project is completed and the service is running, there will be contracts with service levels that need to be met, and monitoring controls will be required to keep up with current standards. At the end of a control's life, this monitoring will lead someone to realize that the control is no longer adequate to protect the service because it has failed for some reason—perhaps hackers have found a way around it, the business needed to change the service in some way that invalidated the control, or you realized that the control was never really effective in the first place. One of the best controls is to avoid having the data in the first place.

Out with the old

One of the most famous marketing slogans of all time is "Don't Mess with Texas," which was developed to reduce the trash that piles up on the sides of roads and highways around the state. Unfortunately, computers are full of digital litter that never goes away. You probably know someone who has more than ten thousand unread email messages in their inbox, or you've seen someone's desktop cluttered with icons of files they never open. These are the examples you see every day. On servers, network drives, cloud storage, and digital file storage, digital litter accumulates and is often forgotten. These files never go away.

Data has a useful lifespan. When the data reaches the end of that useful life, the dangers of it being disclosed or stolen can outweigh the value of keeping it. In some cases, there are requirements that data be kept for certain periods of time. Health records, for example, must be kept for seven years. There is no similar standard for how long email or phone records must be kept. Often, your computer systems allow you to create a process to delete old data automatically when the data reaches the end of its lifetime. Keep in mind that there are also important exceptions to data retention limits. Litigation holds, regulatory requirements, and continuing business needs are just a few of the exceptions to this rule.

Refer to the data inventory you conducted in the literacy section. Review the sample data retention schedule below and determine how long the information in your inventory should be kept. Usually, deleting information is not something that happens on a regular basis, so it's important to establish a regular schedule (monthly, quarterly, annually) with your team or your company to clean out old data. To remind yourself to delete information, treat this task as an annual (or more frequent) spring-cleaning, like you might do in your house. Many local community organizations offer free document-shredding days or electronics-recycling programs where you can destroy information that has collected over time and needs to be destroyed. Below is a sample data retention schedule to help you know how long to keep your personal records:

- Pay stubs and monthly bills—3 years
- Credit card or bank statements—3 years
- Tax information—3 years
- Insurance statements—6 years
- Loan information—6 years
- Warranties or health records—lifetime

Once data has reached the end of its useful life, how do you destroy it? Following are some examples of how to do it, and in parentheses is an estimate of how secure the method is:

- Paper
  - Cross-cut shredding (medium)
  - Burning (high)
- Electronic
  - Rewriting hard drive multiple times (medium)
  - Degaussing (high)
- Online
  - Deleting accounts (low)
  - Using a General Data Protection Regulation (GDPR) Section 17 "forget me" request (high)

The myth of perfect security

One of my employees has a theory. The lock on your front door or the padlock on your locker isn't actually a lock—it's a social contract. When you walk up to a padlocked door, it's like there is a little note from the owner saying that what is behind the lock is his, and he would like you to leave that stuff alone, please. In the physical world, we know locks are ineffective at keeping people out, or people wouldn't invest in lighting, cameras, alarm systems, and ferocious attack lemurs. A padlock can be picked, shimmed, or cut within seconds. A door can be taken off the hinges. You can break a window. There hasn't ever been a lock that couldn't be picked.

The closest the world has ever come to having an unbreakable lock was the Bramah safety lock. Created in 1784 by Joseph Bramah, a polymath engineer living in London, the design would go unpicked for nearly seventy years. Bramah was so confident in his lock design that he painted a challenge on the lock and hung it in his shop window. The winner would receive a prize worth more than $25,000 in today's dollars. He also published detailed design information on how it worked, contrasting with the commonly accepted maxim "Security through obscurity." If picking the lock was impossible, then being completely transparent and open about the details of the lock would only serve to reinforce the strength of the design.

The lock was finally cracked by American locksmith A. C. Hobbs in 1851. Although Bramah had since died, his family agreed to let Hobbs attempt to crack the famous lock. They let him stay upstairs in their London shop and gave him thirty days to crack the lock. It took Hobbs about two weeks. Even though it took two weeks of an expert locksmith working in ideal conditions, once the perception of the lock's impregnability had been broken, people stopped wanting to pay premium prices for almost perfect security when they could get good enough security cheaply in the form of mass-produced locks.

People have a much more difficult time applying the social contract concept when it comes to computers. I think this is in part because to get into another person's computer, I never leave my own keyboard. It is further complicated by the nature of digital information. If I break into your house and steal something, then it is clear that I have violated the social contract. Somehow, it is less clear if I break into your house and make copies of all of your photos. It's still a violation of the social contract, but psychologically, this behavior is more like voyeurism or espionage than theft.

In cybersecurity, the equivalent of the padlock is something called encryption. I won't try to duplicate the very technical descriptions of how encryption works. Encryption is the practice of making it difficult for people other than the intended recipient to eavesdrop on a conversation. Notice I said "difficult," not "impossible." Usually, the strength of encryption can be measured related to the amount of time it takes to decrypt a message. If the length of time it takes to decrypt a message is longer than the information contained in the message needs to remain confidential, the secrecy of the message has been preserved. But encryption is still just like a padlock—it is more of a social contract than a perfect protection. Although in cybersecurity we measure the strength of encryption relative to the number of years it will take to break the encryption, we conveniently forget that the processing power of computers doubles every eighteen months. We conveniently ignore the processing power of governments with massive supercomputers. And we tend to ignore that the keys used to create the encryption in the first place were made by people—and those keys are easy to guess or steal.

It's easy to write off humans as being the weakest link in security, but sometimes they are also the best way to keep something secure. The best example I can give for this is the signs that say "We Card" hanging in grocery and convenience stores across the country. This means that, when buying cigarettes or alcohol, shoppers must produce an identification card that shows they are old enough to make the purchase. In the 1980s, parents could, and sometimes did, send their underage kids on errands to the store—and sometimes these included requests to buy cigarettes. Unfortunately, this meant many kids experimented with smoking at a very early age. This led to passing laws banning the sale of cigarettes from vending machines, ensuring a human had to be involved in the sale process. Checking the identification of the person trying to buy cigarettes to be sure they were an adult became required. If a seller didn't check for ID, the person or the store could face heavy fines from the state or risk losing the ability to sell tobacco products.

Note that states chose to involve a human as a security measure. They could have, for example, automated the checking process by requiring the buyers to swipe their driver's license through a card reader on a vending machine. This might have helped address the issue of fake identification that could potentially trick a human being. Ultimately, humans were involved in this security process so they could use their intelligence to make sure cigarettes were being sold responsibly. Even though it was compulsory and had significant consequences, this solution didn't work perfectly. But it did help address an epidemic of underage smoking while reducing the impact of the health consequences to those kids.

Most companies have employee handbooks that include policies about information privacy and the acceptable use of computers. Compulsory rules have an impact on the culture of the organization. For example, a company may assume that by preventing employees from accessing the internet during work hours, they'll be both more secure and more productive, since employees can't go shopping or waste time on social media while on the clock. Unfortunately, both assumptions would be wrong. The employees could just use their cell phones or set up rogue wireless access points. They also could still be going online and introducing security weaknesses into the company without anyone knowing about it.

Use the Force

Everything you think you know about *Star Wars* is wrong. Adam Shostack wants to change your mind about *Star Wars* to help you understand cybersecurity through a concept he calls threat modeling.[14] When most people think of *Star Wars*, they think of "the Force," a magical ability that encompasses everything from telekinesis to seeing the future. Others think of *Star Wars* as a space opera that tells the story of how the problems of one family changed the course of the galaxy. Still others see George Lucas's opus as nothing more than a hodgepodge of borrowed stories from other genres in a mash-up designed to maximize his ability to sell kids' toys. The truth is much more interesting, at least from a cybersecurity perspective. *Star Wars* is the story of a group of hackers with a political agenda who successfully steal government secrets and use those secrets to topple said government.

Shostack began his career in technology working in health care. At that time, only one university in the world offered a degree program in cybersecurity. This meant Shostack had to learn by talking to people and observing others. While this is true for many early cybersecurity practitioners, the thirst for knowledge is an integral feature of his persona. When Shostack speaks, it is deliberate; he sometimes takes long pauses to genuinely think and reflect before he answers. This is also why his book *Threat Modeling: Designing for Security* is so long. Shostack provides a comprehensive overview of nearly every aspect of cybersecurity, outlining how they all come together in the threat-modeling process. He cites references from the father of modern behavioral economics, Daniel Kahneman, to the Lockheed Martin Cyber Kill Chain. Shostack's career in cybersecurity spans being an entrepreneur and consultant to working for Microsoft. The one common thread in his career involves his approach to designing a security program not based on what data a company has or who is trying to take it away from them but based on what could go wrong.

One of the first things that Shostack tells the people he works with in his consulting practice is that they already know how to use a threat model. Threat modeling is already a part of a person's natural experiences. People intuitively understand how to envision protecting a house and can visualize a bad guy attempting to break in. Similarly, they can imagine a business and understand the challenges of corporate espionage engaged in stealing corporate secrets. They don't need to know what an SQL injection attack is to protect themselves or their businesses. Shostack organizes his approach based on four questions:

- What are we building?
- What could go wrong?
- What will we do about it?
- Did we do a good enough job at answering the first three questions?

These questions are deceptively simple, but the simplicity prevents people from falling into some of their bad habits when it comes to protecting themselves or their companies. These questions are also abstract, which is why Shostack likes to talk about *Star Wars*.

In the *Star Wars* universe, the Galactic Empire is a giant bureaucracy not unlike many large corporations. And, as a bureaucracy, the Empire is the perfect example for illustrating the problems that many of our own companies will face. In the movie *Rogue One*, rebels infiltrate a government data center using stolen credentials, bypassing a giant shield (aka a firewall), to exfiltrate some critical data. They discover a flaw (or vulnerability) in the data that could cause real-world damages. In *A New Hope*, the government responds to this data breach in real time while the hackers try to exploit the vulnerability they've found. The government captures one of the leaders of the hacking coalition, Princess Leia, but she is rescued. The government leaders decide to let her go so they can discover the location of the rest of the hackers, but before they can move in, the hackers use the flaw they discovered to destroy the government's technology.

Shostack wasn't the only person to use *Star Wars* as an analogy for cybersecurity. In 2012 Kellman Meghu, who was the head of Security Engineering for Check Point Software Technologies, gave one of the first presentations that used *Star Wars* to help illustrate cybersecurity concepts. A video of Meghu's talk is available online, complete with videos of the key scenes that illustrate each of the steps in a data breach investigation.[15] Up until Vader walks in, the breach response is going well.

Shostack takes *Star Wars* in a slightly different direction by analyzing how the Empire could have stopped the hack from happening in the first place by better understanding the threats they faced. Perhaps one of the biggest challenges the Galactic Empire must contend with is the overall complexity of managing the security in every aspect of its operation. Most employees only need to know their small part of the world to do their job. The only people who might be able to see the big picture are at the top, and most likely they don't have the time to learn and think about all of the aspects of how the business operates. They must rely on others to know the important parts of their jobs and share what is relevant up the chain of command. Sometimes, internal jockeying for position, politics, and Darth Vader using the Force to physically intimidate his staff tend to distract from the focus needed to respond during a crisis.

Most of the leaders I've worked with during my career have naturally gravitated to taking the same shortcut when it comes to cybersecurity. They ask the question, "What are our peers doing?" In a way, this is a very reasonable approach. By asking this question, you could argue they are crowdsourcing the solution to the problem of having an incomplete understanding of their organization's complexity. Following your peers also provides some legal protection if you can say you were using the industry best practices or standards. This question is also a little dangerous, because who are the right peers to measure yourself against? We need to answer the question specifically—the answer can't be "Google does this, so it must be the right approach."

You must research how organizations of a similar size, in a specific industry, use these controls—and that takes some information sharing between potential competitors. Once you know who your peers are and what they are doing, the other challenge is that your peers may be dealing with legacy systems or processes that are inherently insecure or inefficient. If you had to start your company over from scratch, you might make different choices—and those different choices might be inherently more secure or efficient. Larry Page, the former CEO of Google, argues that the services they build should be ten times better than others. These moonshot ideas often have the advantage of not being held back by prior assumptions, and Page believes the chances of wild successes increase dramatically.

When Shostack formed his company Confidenza Security in 2015, instead of leasing office space and limiting his talent pool, everyone at the company worked from home. Instead of leasing a data center to put servers in, he used freely available cloud services. And yet, complexity was still the enemy. Before the company had a working demo of their product, it took five separate vendors to provide all of the different services just for users to get to the login page. Shostack recalls making the decision to register their business account with Amazon to use two-factor authentication. This required a telephone number. Whose phone number would they use? Would they buy a separate mobile phone just for this purpose? Ultimately, Shostack and his chief technology officer (CTO), both seasoned cybersecurity professionals, agreed this was overkill. If an attacker could fake a two-factor request to the phone, they argued, then the same actor could spoof a text message from Shostack to the CTO or vice versa.

How do you know when you've done enough? There's no silver bullet in terms of controls that can solve every problem every time. Shostack's message is that people are a necessary ingredient in the solutions for our cybersecurity challenges. The first challenge his threat-modeling approach asks people to consider is, essentially, to "know thyself." People must understand not just how the company operates but also how to have empathy for the other people inside the company doing their jobs. Shostack believes that executives must meet security people one-third of the way. Not halfway. This means that cybersecurity professionals must have even more empathy for others. "It's not reasonable for us as security people to require executives to meet us halfway," says Shostack. "If the executive has to meet everyone halfway, there's not time enough in the day for them to do their jobs." Creating a culture that values empathy and empowers individuals to solve problems is one of the most effective ways for a company to protect itself. This is why Culture is the fifth cybersecurity habit.

5

CULTURE

Imagine a scientist looking through a pair of binoculars at a group of primates in a jungle. This scientist has seen many groups of primates living together before, but he notices something for the first time. All the primate groups of this species are the same size. In fact, each species of primate that the scientist observes, including humans, seems to have a limit to the number of members it can include in a group. The most interesting part? This number seems to correlate to the size of the neocortex in the brains of the respective species: the larger the neocortex, the larger the group size. In the early 1990s, a British evolutionary psychologist did just that. He looked at thirty-eight different kinds of primates to calculate the ratio between the size of the group and the size of the neocortex of the animal. He then used this ratio to predict the natural size of a grouping of humans. The psychologist's name was Robin Dunbar, and the number, it turns out, is 148.[1] Dunbar's theory is that it takes a ton of processing power to navigate and maintain the complex relationships inside a group. The more people in a group, the more difficult it is to maintain these relationships.

Several years ago, Facebook did a study on how many "friends" their average user had on the site. Despite having the ability to have nearly limitless numbers of friends, it turns out that this average number was about 150. Facebook began calling this number "Dunbar's number." The average number of friends on Facebook has gone up since then, but the number of friends someone regularly interacts with is quite low.

One of the things the Roman military is best known for is its organizational structure. The size of the unit called a "company" is limited to about 150 soldiers. This structure has been copied by other militaries throughout history, as well as by corporations. The most famous example from the business world is the company Gore-Tex Inc., which limited the number of employees in each of its factories to around 150. Gore-Tex credits this limit with its productivity and efficiency successes. The same numbers hold true for hunter-gatherer societies, Amish parishes, and Christmas card networks, according to Dunbar.

In 1998, on a warm August morning in the desert, I watched from a balcony as my college matriculated the new freshman class. (Matriculation was like a graduation ceremony, except it took place at the beginning of your first year instead of at the end of your final year.) I went to a small liberal arts college, and it was a tradition for the upperclassmen to watch the freshmen walk across the stage and even cheer them on. By the time I graduated, my class contained fewer than seventy people, which meant the whole school had fewer than four hundred undergraduates in total. I loved this because it meant I knew almost everyone.

As I think about Dunbar's number, it helps me to understand what it means to know some people, even if you don't know their name. You might know if they are a smoker. You know who their friends are. You know if they read books in the library or always go to parties or both. You can recognize their gestures, body language, voice, and gait. Maybe you had a class with them. Or maybe you heard them discussing Aristotle in the coffee shop, and you disagreed with their views on metaphysics.

Remembering all these little details turns out to be important. The processing power necessary for developing and maintaining relationships is limited, and your brain can't process everyone equally. So, closer relationships take priority, and you take in their behavioral clues more readily than you do those of strangers. Since you've already spent this mental energy on them, you tend to trust them more than strangers.

In the workplace and the digital world, strangers are everywhere. Sometimes our customers are strangers. Sometimes companies are too big to know even the other employees—maybe you never see the same person twice in the hallway.

The problem at the office is that we can't rely on employee or visitor badges to know who poses a threat. When it comes to email, Facebook, or corporate networks, it's simpler not to trust anyone at all.

Maintaining relationships carries a cognitive cost, and not all relationships are created equally. Dunbar argues there are four layers of people within the limits of his 150-person number, with the inner circles being smaller and more cognitively complex and the outer layers being much larger and requiring less interaction. At the nucleus of Dunbar's circle are your best friends; on average, you have three to five that you interact with at least once per week. The next layer consists of twelve to fifteen close friends you see once per month. Social psychologists call these close friends a "sympathy group," which is why jury trials have twelve members. The next layer, consisting of forty-five to fifty people, is considered distant friends you might see only once per year. The final layer comprises another eighty to eighty-five people you might just be acquaintances with and with whom you have no close interactions. These circles are also important for another reason—they help protect the community's security. As the connections get more distant, and less time is spent interacting with them, those individuals are trusted less, and the security of the core of the community is protected.

The cost of navigating personal relationships, if Dunbar is correct, implies that relationships are the brain's primary purpose. The closer the relationship, the higher the mental cost. This means you can't spend this processing power limitlessly on every interaction you have. With the internet, the various types of electronic communication available to us, and the drastic increase in the number of people we communicate with daily, the question becomes "How can we hope to protect ourselves online if we can only ever trust a small circle of people?"

Biologist Charles Darwin is probably one of the most famous scientists in history, but Darwin was one of two great biologists who emerged in the 1800s. The other was Alfred Russel Wallace. Wallace and Darwin were contemporaries and had corresponded for years, sharing their theories, but Darwin developed his theory of natural selection in secret for nearly twenty years. So, when Wallace shared his ideas about natural selection, Darwin was shocked to see his friend's ideas neatly mirrored his own. They jointly published their papers that year. Wallace disagreed with Darwin when it came to his theories about the brain. Wallace argued other forces than just natural selection were at work.

Wallace argued that, as the human brain evolved, another powerful force changed the structure of the brain: culture. Once humans developed language, both verbal and written, passing along the wisdom of many lifetimes to the next generation became possible.[2] In this way, the human brain became symbiotic with culture. Wallace argued that culture is like the shell of a hermit crab: They form one thing that is greater than what the crab was without it. Instead of a kind of crutch, culture is what has propelled human evolution past the limits of natural selection, making us unique in the animal kingdom.

Wallace's theory provides a clue about how people approach expanding numbers of people when they connect to the internet. When a mind gets to its natural limit of 150 people, it treats them the way its culture has evolved to make it behave. Rather than using existing processing power to manage distant relationships, it uses the historical processing power of brains from the past to navigate those relationships. For example, this can help direct how a person should interact with a stranger on the street asking for directions. It can help you decide whether to accept a connection request on LinkedIn. Our challenge is that our hermit crab shell of culture hasn't had enough time to keep up with the pace of technology. This is why the nine habits mentioned in this book are necessary—to reinforce the structure of the shell.

Both micro- and macro-cultures determine an individual's behavior in different situations. A company may have its own micro-culture that changes the way employees behave when inside or, sometimes, outside the company. Communities may also have their own culture. It may be commonly accepted that a man should remove his hat when inside a church, for example, but this isn't usually also the case inside a shopping mall. Larger cultural influences can vary from city to city or country to country.

The good news is that the micro-culture inside a company can be changed more easily than a macro-culture at the national or international level. Research suggests that only 20 percent of a group of people need to start doing something or refraining from doing something before the group starts to adopt these practices. This is excellent news when it comes to cybersecurity because it means that you don't have to get everyone in a company to change all at once to make a difference. You can start with a smaller, more targeted group and allow culture to spread the message for you. For example, if you adopt the slow-down-and-frown approach I discussed in Chapter 3, you may find people jumping on the bandwagon.

Culture eats cybersecurity for breakfast

Eggo waffles weren't always called Eggo waffles. In the 1950s, during the boom that followed World War II, Americans began a love affair with frozen foods. Frank Dorsa and his three brothers in San Jose, California, were running a popular mayonnaise business and had expanded into powdered waffle mix, but demand for their mix had begun to evaporate. Making waffles was a lot of work.

Dorsa was a bit of an inventor, so he created a giant waffle-making machine using a merry-go-round engine and a number of electric waffle irons. Thousands of waffles were frozen and shipped every day. But their name, the "Froffle" (frozen waffle), was a flop. Instead, customers called the waffles "Eggos," referring to the distinctive egg taste of the Dorsa brothers' mayonnaise. The name, like the waffles, stuck around.

The Kellogg Company bought the Eggo waffles line in 1968, and four years later they introduced the slogan "L'Eggo My Eggo." The marketing campaign was one of the most successful of all time, running continuously for thirty-six years. The commercials depicted kids and parents in an escalating struggle to maintain possession of their precious frozen waffles. The message was clear: The waffles were so good that, if you weren't careful, someone might steal them from you.

In my conversations with CISOs and chief information officers (CIOs) from across the country, I've learned CISOs are expected to create a "culture" of security. One person can't create a culture, nor can one person acting alone change a culture that already exists. Leadership guru Peter Drucker is widely credited with creating the phrase "Culture eats strategy for breakfast." Drucker's message is that an organization's culture is much more powerful in creating success than the individual strategies the executives come up with to drive an organization forward. To be clear, strategy is important. But when an organization values empathy and empowerment, where employees take responsibility for their own results and where innovation is fostered, the company has a greater chance of success.

Just like delicious waffles, culture also eats cybersecurity for breakfast.

Cybersecurity culture is only one facet of an organization's overall culture; it must be considered part of a larger whole before it can change. For example, a company may have a high-pressure culture where employees are expected to respond to an email instantly. What hope is there that they'll identify and respond to red flags in phishing messages if this culture is in place? On the other hand, what if the industry or the job is so competitive that changing that aspect of the culture would mean going out of business? Essentially, Drucker's advice insists we should have empathy for our employees. Blaming hardworking people for our cybersecurity woes can blind us to this.

If it's true that culture eats cybersecurity for breakfast, then testing this theory should be possible. If the theory is true, then a company with a poor culture, no matter how much they focus on cybersecurity, would be hacked or breached more by rogue insiders or individuals not following policy or controls more often. The website Glassdoor lets current and former employees of companies post ratings from one to five stars and write reviews about what working at a company was like, which provides a simplified method for measuring culture. Comparing the Glassdoor ratings of a company like Equifax and its competitors, TransUnion and Experian, provides a great case study. Equifax as of early 2020 has a Glassdoor rating of 2.9, while TransUnion's rating sits at 3.9 and Experian's is 3.7. I should note here that Equifax's rating two years earlier was a 3.4 and has declined steadily, while TransUnion's and Experian's have both risen.

To further test this theory, I looked at the Glassdoor ratings of nearly four hundred companies that have been breached in the last year and found that their ratings are noticeably lower than the average rating for others in the same industry. Perhaps more troubling, companies with a rating from 3.0 to 3.4 are three times more likely to have been breached than those with a rating above 4.0. None of the companies that had multiple breaches in the last year had a rating above 4.0. This doesn't mean that a company with a low rating will automatically be breached. There are many reasons why a company with good security and a great culture might get breached—perhaps the company is just a bigger target. This list also doesn't account for companies that have been hacked but haven't realized it yet. Still, these numbers demonstrate how a company's overall culture plays a significant role in cybersecurity.

At its core, cybersecurity is a leadership issue. The apparent correlation between Glassdoor rankings and breaches provides another indicator regarding the truth in Drucker's wisdom on culture. And this correlation provides even more incentive for us to improve not just our cybersecurity but our overall culture. To borrow a quote from Benjamin Franklin, "We must, indeed, all hang together, or most assuredly we shall all hang separately."[3]

Mandy Price worked for her law firm for eleven years, and no one in the office knew what her real hair looked like or what her real name was. Price's given name is Mandisa. She's a smart, dedicated attorney who graduated from Harvard Law. She's also African American. She participated in several diversity and inclusion initiatives at the firms where she worked. She chaired a committee. But the real change for her came when she realized the people she now considered friends didn't really know who she was. Price left her firm and started a company, Kanarys, to help make a real difference when it comes to diversity. Many organizations have sensitivity training. Some conduct surveys to help measure inclusiveness and track improvements over time. Kanarys uses machine learning to analyze survey responses to look for potential anomalies and find deviations inside a company, among competitors, or in the industry. But the firms that Price works with at Kanarys don't stop there. Price also asks her clients to sign a pledge and make a commitment allowing everyone to be their real selves while unlocking their full potential. According to a 2017 McKinsey & Company study, diverse companies are more profitable than their counterparts.[4] Companies in the top quartile of gender diversity on their executive teams were 21 percent more profitable. Companies in the top quartile of ethnic diversity on their executive teams were 35 percent more profitable.

Before we start to think about changing our culture, we need to understand several things about our organizations. We need to use Big Data to figure out the right things to look for to change our security outcomes.

What would a cybersecurity culture audit look like? Just like Mandy Price with diversity, we need to conduct surveys and ask essential questions about what cybersecurity looks like inside our organizations. Are security and safety discussed? Is someone responsible for security? Are employees asked to participate in inspections? Is there a process for reporting security concerns or suggestions? How often are exceptions to policy requested?

An elephant never forgets

You've probably heard the phrase "An elephant never forgets." And it's true. Elephants have an amazing memory. As the largest land mammal, they have a massive brain. They can remember other elephants or watering holes for decades. But there is a downside to this memory. I remember learning as a child that if an elephant is chained up as a baby, they would remember that they can't escape for the rest of their lives. So, even when they are fully grown, they can be restrained with just a small rope. People, as it turns out, have the same propensity to resign themselves to their situations.

Over the last decade, using functional magnetic resonance imaging (fMRI) scanners, researchers have probed the neuroscience and psychology of fear versus happiness. None of those researchers is more famous than the psychologist Martin Seligman. Today, he is known as the father of positive psychology, but in the 1960s, Seligman was working on the problem of depression. His research attempted to replicate depression in animals so he could study and understand it. But an unusual thing happened; the animals in his early studies didn't just become depressed. They became helpless. When the animals realized they couldn't escape or do anything to stop the experiment, they stopped trying. Seligman called this phenomenon "learned helplessness," and he went on to demonstrate that humans, too, exhibit this same problem when exposed to stress.

But Seligman went further; he wanted to know if the subjects could unlearn their helplessness and, thus, become healthy subjects again— which could lead to improvements in depression treatments. His team of researchers tried all the tricks in the book, but nothing worked. So, they did what experimenters don't normally do . . . they intervened. When Seligman and his colleagues physically showed the animals they could escape or stop the experiment, the helplessness eventually went away. But once wasn't enough; the researchers needed to intervene at least twice, if not multiple times, before the animals changed their behaviors.[5]

This insight is incredibly important for organizations and communities looking to change their cultures from fear and helplessness to hope and empowerment. Alone, we can't change. We need help. And that help can't stop until the transformation is complete. This last part is difficult because we expect humans to learn and move on. We sometimes attribute needing help more than once to weakness. We use the derogatory term "hand-holding" for people who require this constant attention. But just like with Drucker's advice, this is the point at which we need to have the most empathy for others so they can start believing change is possible.

As a CISO, I've found several activities that can help you begin moving from a culture of fear to a culture of hope while strengthening your security culture along the way.

Stakeholder meetings

One CISO I work with met with the top fifty stakeholders in his company during his first few months on the job. This sets the tone of your relationship moving forward and gives you the opportunity to create expectations and build partnerships. It also gives you the opportunity to understand the existing culture of the organization.

Employee orientation

When any new employee starts in our organization, I meet with them in person for at least thirty minutes to talk about security. This moves security into the foreground of the things they think about as they're learning the culture of their new environment, and it sets the expectation that the organization cares about security. Over time, this can dramatically shift the culture of the organization.

Kaizen days

Toyota was the first to adopt the Kaizen approach of continuous improvement into its culture. Kaizen days are like company holidays where employees are asked to focus on improving processes. This concept doesn't have to be limited to just process improvements, however. Some organizations have used this to help improve cybersecurity processes, as well.

Competitions

Many organizations look for ways to "gamify" security. One method for doing this is to create a competition to identify phishing emails, for example. Competition creates a strong motivation to change.

Baked-in security

Security tends to be an afterthought, and consequently, it must be "bolted on" after a product is designed or a project is complete. This can be addressed by building relationships with project managers or departments to ensure security is engaged from the beginning of any project or initiative. In his book *The Phoenix Project*, Gene Kim, the creator of the DevOps movement, suggests that security team members be added by default to every project so they can act as consultants in partnership with the business rather than obstacles to meeting objectives later.

Clean desk policy

Some organizations have adopted what is called a clean desk policy. A clean desk policy requires employees to move paper off desks and into locked cabinets at the end of each day. This prevents accidental loss of information if someone gains access to your office. Studies have also shown that a clean desk can make employees more productive, saving them several hours per week normally spent looking for lost papers and allowing them to focus on one task at a time.

Token reminders

Law enforcement and the Department of Defense are two examples of organizations that use "challenge coins" to commemorate participation in special events or responses. This gives the recipient a physical token to remember the event and help motivate future positive behaviors. These tokens can also act as conversation pieces to help motivate the behavior of others. At Southern Methodist University, I presented superhero capes with the university logo on them to our cybersecurity superheroes. Many folks still have those capes in their offices and continue to talk about them when people come to visit years later.

Incentives

Offering incentives for security is a powerful motivator. Some companies I've spoken to offer bonuses, while others take bonuses away if a breach has occurred. Even small rewards, like gift cards or extra vacation time, can motivate staff members to put some extra effort toward reaching goals or establishing good habits.

The security minute

Setting aside the first minute of every meeting to reinforce the importance of cybersecurity goes a long way toward shifting your culture toward security.

Recognition

When people start to participate in security, keep that participation going by recognizing their efforts. This can be as simple as a thank-you note, email, or shout-out to the team. You can include their names and stories in newsletters or pass along praise to their supervisors. I've done annual award ceremonies for people who participated in programs, both inside and outside of IT.

Spring-cleaning events

One of the challenges in large organizations is the paper and digital litter that accumulates over time. As discussed in Chapter 4, data has a useful life cycle but can become a liability when it is no longer needed. Having an annual cleanout serves the purpose of providing a time to destroy old documents while also reinforcing the expectation that employees should be deleting data when it's no longer needed.

Humans, like elephants, dogs, and other animals, experience learned helplessness when they are inside large organizations. The larger the organization, the more easily this can happen due to bureaucracy, politics, and other forces at play. Taking the time to organize the activities listed above can help send a message that individuals and their ideas and values are significant to the organization. And if someone cares, it's more likely that the individual can unlearn their helplessness. But there is also something that we as individuals can do to help change organizations from the inside out. Rather than the structured approach that a corporation might take, when individuals are in charge of culture, it looks a lot more random.

Random acts of security

In 1982 writer Anne Herbert originated the phrase "random acts of kindness." With more and more violent crime being reported in the news, Herbert wanted to create a wave of kindness to counteract the vicious cycle of negativity. The hope was that if enough people performed random acts, like buying coffee for a stranger or allowing someone to merge into traffic, a virtuous cycle of positivity would be created instead, making the world a better place.

University of California psychologist Sonja Lyubomirsky examined the idea of random acts of kindness in a study that concluded in 2005.[6] The study didn't focus on making the world a better place but on whether the practice of kindness would have an impact on making people happy. It worked. This practice is one of the most effective ways of making people happy. But there was a trick. The practice isn't really random. At night, subjects had to create a plan for what they would do to be kind in certain situations, so when the opportunity came up, they could take it. The subject's intentionality greatly influenced their outcomes. The greater the intention, the bigger the result—at least in the short term. The other significant factor was the variety of acts planned and engaged in during the week. Variety helped cement long-term, lasting effects.

Corporate awareness programs can benefit from incorporating random acts of security.

Every company must incorporate great cybersecurity awareness training to help employees protect themselves and the company from hackers. CISOs do a good job informing employees about risks, but users have difficulty integrating the practices we teach them into their daily lives. One of the most effective techniques for helping them is to practice random acts of security.

Each day, at random, you should perform one intentional action to make your environment more secure, at home, at work, or in the community. It's important to identify the action you will perform each day before doing it, instead of noting the act afterward. To benefit the most from this exercise, the act you perform must be intentional but also different enough from an individual's daily routine that they notice it.

At the end of your security training, challenge your employees to perform at least one—or more—acts of security per day:

- Introduce the "security minute" at the beginning of meetings.

- Challenge someone "tailgating" through a secured door without using their card access.

- Instead of clicking on a link, go directly to the website or call the sender to ensure the message was really from them.

- Establish a clean desk policy. Always remove papers from your desk before you leave at the end of each day.

- If you see a computer that isn't locked with a password, lock it and leave a note.

One of a CISO's most challenging tasks is changing their organization's culture toward being more security-centric. Most approaches come from the top down and focus on enforcing compliance but do little to create a culture of security. You must have leadership support to grow a successful security program—but remember, culture eats cybersecurity for breakfast. Performing random acts of cybersecurity is a way of providing grassroots support for your program from the bottom up. Practicing this strategy will help your employees develop a security mindset and give people the chance to believe they can make a difference. And, given that chance, they will.

Deputizing to create purpose

Can we do anything to make this the year we finally reduce cybercrime? In his book *The Purpose Driven Life*, Pastor Rick Warren writes, "The truth is, almost everything we do is done poorly when we start doing it—that's how we learn." Cybersecurity is about getting better. To succeed, we need to believe success is possible. I suggest that, like the title of Pastor Warren's book, we need to have more than belief. To succeed, we require purpose.

In the 1990s, Dr. Mark Muraven, now a professor of psychology at the University of Albany, State University of New York, wanted to know whether willpower is a competency—something that can be learned and mastered. If I can wait fifteen minutes for an Oreo today, will I always be able to wait for that Oreo, just like I can always pick up a bike and ride it once I've learned? Muraven thought that there was something else going on, because, in his experience, some days were different than others. This makes sense to me. Some days I'm excited about writing, and other days I get distracted more easily.

According to Muraven, more than two hundred studies about willpower have been conducted, and they've all come to the same conclusion. "[Willpower] isn't a skill," Muraven observed. "It's a muscle, like the muscles in our arms or legs, and it gets tired as it works harder, so there's less power left over for other things."[7]

Unlike traditional muscles, willpower isn't just taxed by the effort of delaying gratification. In a later test, Muraven looked at the impact emotions have on willpower. Half the subjects were asked warmly and politely what the test was about, and they were asked for their feedback after the test. The researchers were rude to the other half, and the reason for the test was never explained to them. The subjects whose "willpower muscles" had been strained, not just by the test but by stress from the environment, performed poorly when compared to their unperturbed counterparts. The same is true for our cybersecurity muscles. When they are taxed by other things in the environment, it's harder to accomplish our security goals.

Does this sound like a school or office environment you've heard of before? A teacher or manager barking orders? Playing favorites? Not explaining the overall goal of a project?

Muraven observed that if the test's subjects thought they were participating for personal reasons, if they felt like it was a choice or something they enjoyed because it helped someone else, it was much less taxing on their willpower. This makes sense: If someone forced you to exercise, you probably wouldn't work as hard as you would if you were trying to lose weight or raise money for charity. The lesson for cybersecurity is also clear. If our employees are just following orders, their security muscles get tired much faster. If they feel like what they do doesn't matter or that they can't make a difference, it takes significant amounts of security horsepower to do the same tasks, be it not sharing passwords or not clicking on phishing messages.

Incentivizing good behavior is important, but creating a culture that moves beyond incentives to give employees purpose is what will make the biggest difference in your cybersecurity program. This means your employees must be empowered to make decisions of consequence. This is why having tools that give everyone, not just cybersecurity professionals, a chance to get timely, relevant information is so important. I call this process deputizing your staff, and there are important implications on both sides of the relationship. Deputizing your staff empowers employees by giving them roles to play, but it also requires leadership to acknowledge that employees have the authority to make decisions.

What does deputizing people for cybersecurity look like? I think giving people purpose requires more than just putting up posters with "See Something. Say Something" written on them. Here are some ideas:

- Ask for help. Provide a channel where people can report potential security issues, including suspicious email or activity. Offer suggestions to help improve their business practices, like how to securely handle sensitive information.

- Create an internal security advisory council and make that team a real part of your security governance. Let them help create organization-wide security risk registers and prioritize risks to manage.

- Create a cybersecurity newsletter to share real stories about how cybercriminals have affected the business. Take this opportunity to tell stories of customers or employees who were affected.

Putting a face behind the people you're helping creates a human connection to security.

- Regularly conduct breach drills for everyone in the company, just like fire drills, to encourage employee awareness regarding your procedures. Assign departmental captains to help organize and report on progress.

- Create an award program for employees (not just in IT) that recognizes employees for their contributions to cybersecurity.

- Recognize and give credit to people for being a part of reporting or helping respond to an incident. Have a shout-out email list to these people, or include them in a newsletter with their pictures.

Purpose plays a critical role in changing habits because it provides the motivation to make a lasting difference. You must have a purpose to quit smoking, to lose weight, or to eat healthy. While these are all noble aspirations, the activities in and of themselves aren't enough to make lasting changes. If they were, there wouldn't be a billion-dollar industry around quitting smoking, and bookstores wouldn't be full of diet books.

In Chapter 3, I talked about using incentives to help change behaviors in cybersecurity. I hope that more companies will find ways to incentivize security. As we have the conversation about incentives, we must also understand that incentives will only go so far toward improving cybersecurity. Incentives will change some behaviors. But incentives, by themselves, won't create a culture of security. What we need to do, like what Pastor Warren describes in his book, is to go beyond incentives to create purpose-driven security.

Keeping purpose top of mind

In 1847 the infant mortality rate at Dr. Ignaz Semmelweis's hospital was 18.3 percent. One out of every five children died after they were born, and no one knew why. But Semmelweis made it his mission to save as many lives as he could. At the time, doctors didn't know about germs or bacteria or how they were transmitted from one person to another. But Semmelweis noticed something important—drastically fewer babies died after being delivered by midwives at home rather than by doctors at his hospital. He spent the next several days watching the doctors deliver babies and saw something that would change hospital work forever. Doctors frequently went directly from the autopsy room to the delivery room without washing their hands in between. Semmelweis began requiring that every intern in the delivery ward wash their hands before delivering a baby. In just two months, the mortality rate dropped to under 2 percent—reducing infant deaths by nearly 90 percent.[8]

Almost every movie or TV show about doctors features them going through an intricate process of scrubbing their hands. The actors then hold their hands up to dry while avoiding touching anything until the surgery. Unfortunately, in this case, life does not imitate art. In hospitals around the country, getting doctors and nurses to wash their hands enough is still a challenge. According to a 2011 study by the Centers for Disease Control, the compliance rate for handwashing at hospitals and nursing homes is less than 50 percent nationwide.[9] Numerous research studies over the past twenty years have tried to discover why this is and what can be done about it. One answer, as it turns out, is to remind doctors and nurses of their purpose. The response to the COVID-19 pandemic in 2020 has created a shared global purpose for saving lives, not just for handwashing in the medical community, but the lessons on how to improve our response continue to pour in.

Dr. David Hofmann is a professor of leadership and organizational behavior at the University of North Carolina at Chapel Hill. He and study coauthor, Dr. Adam Grant, took measurements of how much soap was being used at each handwashing station in a large North Carolina hospital.[10] Hofmann and Grant then placed three different signs in front of those handwashing stations. The first was the control and stated, "Gel In, Wash Out." The next sign said, "Hand

Hygiene Prevents You From Catching Diseases." The final sign read, "Hand Hygiene Prevents Patients From Catching Diseases." The patient-focused sign produced a 33 percent increase in handwashing over two weeks. Doctors and nurses give several reasons for not washing their hands: They were carrying too much, it dries out their skin, or they were too busy. Because doctors and nurses get sick less frequently, they don't believe they need to wash their hands, even though numerous studies have shown that when handwashing goes up, infection rates go down. Hofmann and Grant wanted to see if they could help the doctors to stop thinking about themselves, focusing on the patients instead. Hofmann thinks this works because it reflects the oath all doctors take to do no harm to their patients.

If you have kids, you'll know they need constant reminders to take baths and brush their teeth. This normal part of parenting can help us understand how to improve our cybersecurity culture as well. For basic routines to become habitual, we must regularly remind ourselves to perform them. Because many of these cybersecurity routines, like updating your phone, are only performed a few times a year (if they're performed at all), it's sometimes difficult to build these habits.

To change behavior, you need several things. According to Charles Duhigg, author of the *New York Times* best seller *The Power of Habit*, you need to understand the unconscious routines we regularly follow. To break a bad habit, you must understand the cues that trigger our unconscious behavior to replace bad behaviors with good ones. You need to create a reward after those good behaviors are in place to induce a craving that establishes a loop to get those behaviors to repeat. In the case of the surgeons in the study above, the cue was the poster. This cue led to them replacing a bad behavior (not washing their hands) with a good one. And the reward was the reminder of the connection between the doctors and their commitment to serving their patients. In cybersecurity, there is also a danger that we will forget our basic hygienic behaviors like changing passwords or patching our computers. The implication from the surgeon research is that to be effective, we need to remind ourselves of who we are protecting by including pictures of our customers or those in our community.

Cybersecurity isn't just one thing; it's nine different habits we all follow to some degree or another. Mastering the nine habits requires that you follow Duhigg's advice for each habit individually. You need to find the cue, replace the bad routines that follow with good habits, then reward yourself.

Habits become hardwired into your brain. The neuroscience behind this is still in its infancy, but two brain functions seem to foster habits being built: First, you start thinking faster, and then you stop "thinking" at all.

Brain activity transmits electrical signals from one part of the brain to another. As you repeat a certain activity over time, your brain undergoes a change. A layer of fatty tissue called a myelin sheath forms around the nerve axons. The myelin sheath insulates the axon and increases the rate at which information travels along the nerve. The implication is that your brain gets faster by repeating behaviors. This makes these actions "feel" easier as time goes on, meaning you are more likely to repeat them time after time.

Keep repeating those actions, however, and the brain starts to rewire itself further, delegating the actions out of the parts of the brain that control conscious thought.

In the 1990s, a team of researchers at MIT conducted a series of experiments to monitor the basal ganglia, a tiny spiral-shaped structure between the forebrain and midbrain. They monitored rats' brains as they ran through mazes to monitor where the problem-solving of the maze was taking place. The first time the rats ran the maze, the brain scans lit up the entire time they searched for their reward—chocolate.[11] After a week of running the maze, the scans hardly showed any activity except for one place—the basal ganglia. If you've ever arrived at work so immersed in thought you don't remember driving to the office, this is what happened: Essentially, your basal ganglia took over all of the actions necessary for driving, freeing up your neocortex to think about really important things, like planning for a meeting or making an upcoming deadline.

Unfortunately, the basal ganglia also may be running your brain on autopilot when you're clicking on a link in an email while you're listening to a conference call. This means we need to be aware and deliberate about the work habits we create for ourselves.

Research varies on how long it takes to build a habit, as anyone who has gone on a diet or resolved to exercise will tell you. But just like with the rats, a little bit of chocolate can be a nice motivator. Waiting weeks to build up to an extravagant celebration isn't as effective as immediate gratification. Duhigg suggests giving yourself a small reward for each step you take. For example, treat yourself to your favorite candy or spend a minute looking at your favorite picture as a reward as you work toward reaching your goal. This is the role incentives can help play. Incentives that offer fast dopamine hits on a more regular basis will provide greater reinforcement to change behaviors, and this can be effective for mastering all nine cybersecurity habits. And expensive incentives aren't necessarily the most effective means for change. The incentives that mean the most to you are.

Build a culture of hope

"It's impossible to hack my system," said one of the other lab administrators to Stuart McClure. A teaching assistant in a computer lab at the University of Colorado at Boulder, Stuart had discovered the remnants of the Morris worm on one of the computers he had been administering, left there by a project from a former administrator.[12] He had never heard of the Morris worm, but he thought it was cool that someone could write a program that could take down one-third of the computers on the internet by taking advantage of features built into the operating system. The other admin was making fun of Stuart and his insecure lab, so Stuart, after asking permission to attempt to hack his computers, asked what he would win if he were successful. "A beer," the other admin responded.

Stuart stayed up for two nights, discovered the encryption algorithm to the other TA's password file, and wrote a brute-force algorithm in the C programming language to find his encrypted password hash. In a cybersecurity context, a hash is a string of characters that represents a different piece of information, such as a password, an email, or a file. Hashes are used as a substitute for the original data. Sometimes hashes can be reverse engineered to recreate the original data, in this case the password of the other TA. At the end of the next day, Stuart wrote several characters down on a piece of paper and passed it to the overconfident lab admin. "Is this your password?" Stuart asked. It was.

Stuart then began writing articles about hacking techniques, similar to a magician going against the code and revealing to the public how magic tricks were accomplished. Stuart was fascinated and wanted to document them. He cataloged these techniques to test against new products. Over time, he compiled these into the first book I ever read on cybersecurity, *Hacking Exposed*. Now in its seventh edition, *Hacking Exposed* has sold more than five hundred thousand copies worldwide and has spawned a series of other hacking guides.[13] "You have to know how a burglar gets into your house to prevent a burglar," Stuart said.

Stuart cofounded the security consulting company Foundstone before becoming the global chief technology officer for McAfee. As cofounder and former CEO of Cylance, a company that says it has found the "cure" for malware and execution-based cyberattacks, Stuart wasn't just using his years of experience in the hacking world to help secure companies. He was using his years of experience to create a different kind of company.

In a way, Stuart's career has come full circle. From that initial challenge from the other computer lab technician who thought that it was impossible for his computer to be hacked, we've come to a place where people in the security community assume everything will eventually be hacked. At conferences and in boardrooms throughout the world, you hear the phrase "It's a matter of when, not if." Stuart is trying to make us believe that it's possible to get back to the place where we've got an earned confidence that we can actually prevent security breaches from happening.

Friday, May 12, 2017, was shaping up to be a really nice day. I was going to have lunch at a gourmet fried chicken restaurant with a colleague, the weather was perfect, and I had no meetings on my calendar—until a ransomware campaign infected computers all over the world, creating global headlines. Ransomware is a type of computer virus that infects computers and encrypts all the files on them, effectively making them unusable. Once a computer is infected, the user has two choices: Pay the ransom or reinstall an operating system and start from scratch—and hopefully, the computer had a backup, so the files, family photos, emails, or other work the user had on the computer can be restored.

On the day of the first outbreak of the ransomware variant known as WannaCry, while newspapers and websites all over the world were tallying up the costs, computer security firms were sending email blasts with basically the same message: "If you had bought our product, you would have been safe. So, now would be a really good time to buy our product." This has been a common refrain for the last twenty years in cybersecurity: Vendors use fear to sell their products, and CISOs and CIOs use fear to get money to buy those same products.

Stuart's approach was different. Cylance didn't send any marketing messages touting the success of its products because Cylance doesn't use fear to sell them. Instead, on the day WannaCry came out, the company sent an email to current customers indicating it had done regression testing of different versions of its software covering the past eighteen months and had found that its artificial intelligence-based antivirus product would have protected its customers not just from WannaCry but from the zero-day vulnerability that WannaCry used to infect computers, more than a year before the zero-day vulnerability was announced to the public. But they didn't use this in their marketing.

From the beginning, Cylance made a conscious decision not to use FUD (fear, uncertainty, and doubt) to pitch their solutions. "We're not going to sell on fear. We're going to sell on hope," Stuart said. "Hope that you can actually prevent this stuff from happening." Selling on fear is good in the short term, Stuart explains, but if your product actually works, you won't get hacked. And if you sell using fear and those fears never materialize, then you look like the boy in the Aesop fable who cried wolf. People lose trust in you, and they won't listen when it really matters.

Stuart's message of selling not through fear but through hope paid off, by the way. At the end of 2018, his company was acquired by BlackBerry for $1.4 billion,[14] making Cylance one of the rare unicorns Silicon Valley investors dream of.

Once you begin to establish a strong cybersecurity culture, different people inside your organization will begin to take more active roles in performing security routines. However, when lots of people start working together, they need to coordinate their activities to be successful. This coordination requires a plan. And a plan is one of the things that the habit of Diligence gives you.

6

DILIGENCE

Shawn Tuma was sitting in his new office, arms crossed, staring at the ceiling. A blond-haired Texan who spoke slowly and deliberately and was known for wearing boots instead of wingtips, Tuma was a second-year attorney at Vial, Hamilton, Koch & Knox, a large law firm based in Dallas. He had just moved into his new office, so he hadn't hung his diplomas on the walls. His papers were all still in boxes. One of the senior attorneys in the office stopped in the doorway and asked, "What are you doing?"

After several seconds Tuma responded, "Thinking."

"You can't bill for thinking," the partner said and walked away.

Lawyers can't bill for thinking. They can bill for reviewing documents. They can bill for preparing memos. They can bill for depositions or negotiations with opposing counsel. But what they must never do is bill for thinking. Why? Because the clients will tear up the bill and say, "We aren't paying you to daydream."

The great irony here is that every client hires their attorney to think. Clients need someone to understand their problems and help come up with solutions. Why is there this disconnect between what lawyers do and what they get paid to do? Why is thinking perceived as something you should do on your own time? The answer, it seems, boils down to not being able to see or quantify the outcomes of deep and careful consideration. What you can see are reports, memos, and charts. There's no distinction between thinking about what the report should say versus having done the report. The quality of the report is usually attributed to the natural talent of the person who delivered it rather than the amount of time they spent thinking about the problem.

Diligence is the habit of taking time to think. When we practice cybersecurity diligence, we plan for what to do when something goes wrong. We prepare for many kinds of events depending on who we are and what we're trying to protect, which requires that we understand secrecy and we know what controls we can put in place to protect ourselves. Cybersecurity diligence includes having a plan in place that we revise when necessary, learning from our mistakes, implementing the right kind of training, and being proactive. When we are diligent about cybersecurity, we take the time to think.

While Tuma was still in law school, one of his professors gave out a writing assignment. The class was to participate in a directed research project where the students would research legal issues that might be important in the next two to three years. The project was to write a publishable law review paper by the end of the class. Tuma wrote on the legal implications of Y2K. The year was 1998, and national headlines were already talking about how many computers had a flaw where they hadn't been designed to run starting in the year 2000—this was known as the Millennium Bug. The fear was that every computer in the world would just shut down, sending society back into the Dark Ages. Tuma's paper was titled "It Ain't Over Till . . ."

Looking two to three years into the future to determine what the next wave of issues would be like defined Tuma's legal career. He spent years becoming an expert in those areas right when they became relevant. Thinking ahead allowed him to be prepared, an essential element in diligence. This gave him a head start on his career and helped him advance as an attorney through his various firms. This is what led him to technology law.

Tuma foresaw issues regarding electronic contracts and signatures. Then he began specializing in computer fraud and hacking. He became a founding member of the CyberAvengers, a group of cybersecurity professionals that came together to provide free expert resources and guides, including their *#CyberAvengers Playbook*, which allows others to get a head start on their own diligence. Tuma's career has been defined by his mastery of the habit of diligence. Diligence allows you to be prepared so that when you come upon a challenge, you can control your own destiny instead of reacting and letting the situation control you.

One of the driving forces in my own career has been the desire to change organizations from being reactive to proactive. Being reactive means doing something without giving yourself time to think, to be diligent. You're only responding to what someone else has thought about. "Businesses can spend days or weeks responding to cybersecurity incidents like ransomware," says Tuma. "And that's time they aren't making their business more profitable." Tuma often gets calls immediately after a customer has experienced an issue to help walk them through their response, and he helps them build a plan for next time. Tuma's goal is to work himself out of a job by making sure all of his clients embrace the habit of diligence.

Have a plan in place

In the early 1990s, Sheina Orbell had just received her doctorate and started her career in research. She received a prestigious fellowship in 1992 from the UK's Medical Research Council and began a project on elderly knee and hip replacement patients. Orbell isn't a surgeon or an orthopedist, however; she is a psychologist, and she wanted to understand how much of the healing process was mental and how much was physical. So, she went to Scotland and recruited a group of elderly patients, mostly in their late sixties, to find out. Patients who have had these types of surgeries must endure extremely painful rehabilitation and must start moving again as soon as they wake after surgery. Patients who quit rehab early are at an increased risk of death due to a blood clot.

Orbell's project was simple. She gave each patient a blank note-book. Her instructions were equally simple. Patients were required to fill in each page with their recovery goals for the week. During the study, the patients wrote about how they would handle their pain in specific situations, like when they were required to walk to a bus stop, and what pills they would need to take if the pain became too much. This simple process led to an incredible outcome. After three months, the patients who had completed writing the goals were able to get out of their wheelchair unassisted three times faster and had started to walk twice as fast as the other patients.[1] By writing down a plan, the patients exerted a measure of control over their own situation and were prepared to handle the pain when it came.

Just like with these patients, keeping a journal about what you will do, and writing down your goals for how you will handle future situa-tions, can lead to dramatic changes in your preparedness. Ask yourself what you might do if you get a scam phone call on your cell phone. What would you do if your computer crashed and you lost your infor-mation? What if you forgot a password and couldn't get access to an account? Research has shown that writing in a journal will reinforce your experiences, so you learn from them faster than if you hadn't written anything at all. When it comes to cybersecurity, even a small amount of preparation can make a dramatic difference.

Each time you test the plan, or even when you go through a real-life incident, you should conduct a lessons-learned review to debrief on the event. Did the response go as planned? What surprises were encountered? What worked well and what could have been improved upon? What metrics can you track to review how you are doing? After your lessons-learned exercise, you should review your cyberse-curity plan and revise it accordingly. Consider changes to the threat environment, new techniques or attacks being targeted, or new vul-nerabilities in your program. Your plan should never be static. A security plan should be reviewed and revised, even if only slightly, at least once per year.

When Tuma looks at the future of cybersecurity, he sees one thing that can make the biggest difference—thinking. The person designated to lead the cybersecurity program needs to act more like a coach than someone who just runs the technology that supports cybersecurity. Having this coach in place is a vital part of preparedness. Tuma says, "In security, we hear about the big issues being lack of funding or lack of talent. I'm not seeing that be the biggest problem. I'm seeing companies spending money on tools they don't know how to use or services they don't need because they don't have a head coach, they don't have someone seeing the whole playing field, understanding how it all fits together, how the team works together, and seeing the flow of the game. They're missing the obvious easy stuff because nobody's seeing the big picture. Everyone is busy doing, and nobody is stepping back to think."

I have a small team of engineers at Southern Methodist University (SMU). Like many other universities our size, we only have six cybersecurity staff members. When I talk about my cybersecurity team, I say that I have twenty-five hundred employees. A team of six could never be expected to secure every aspect of security for thousands of computers spread over a campus the size of a square mile. Every employee is responsible for the security not just of their computer but of the data they have access to. They make decisions about clicking on potential phishing links and on whether to choose a vendor that supports encryption. They decide when to call for help and when to figure things out for themselves. For years, it's been said that security is everyone's job. As I realized how decentralized our security program really was, I knew I couldn't be successful unless I thought of myself less as the controller of all of these decisions and more as the coach of a team of people working together to solve problems.

If an incident were to happen tomorrow, it's already too late to try and figure out how to respond, who to call, or whether to bring in help. In the heat of the moment, people need a written, commonsense set of directions about how to react. In other words, they need a plan. One of the best ways to help people have the appropriate reaction in the moment is to make sure they've not only seen the plan but practiced it. Cybersecurity diligence consists of the plans, contacts, and contracts put in place to prepare for when, not if, secret information is exposed.

Cybersecurity habits are individual acts. To be effective, these individual acts of the business, institution, or community need to be coordinated into one cohesive whole. Learning how to plan is possible, but just like anything else, it takes practice. This is why things like tabletop exercises are so important. The primary focus of your cybersecurity plan should be preparing for a breach as though it is inevitable. Each individual act you take fits into the larger picture of protecting yourself, your family, or your company from threats.

Experience is the best teacher

Often, the most diligent CISOs I know wear data breaches they've experienced as a badge of honor. Are there things that they would have done differently? Of course! And that's the point. They've been through something that others just haven't experienced, and they've learned tremendous lessons along the way about what they'd do differently next time. And diligent companies, in the words of Winston Churchill, "never waste a good crisis" and take that opportunity to improve themselves. It turns out that getting better before an incident and getting better after an incident aren't mutually exclusive. Getting better before an incident can help you make sure you don't let the crisis go to waste afterward.

I was eavesdropping on two people at a conference last year. They were discussing a recent security incident that had happened at the woman's company. "He should be fired" was the other person's immediate response. Firing should be the last resort, not a default response. From what I gleaned from their conversation, the offense didn't really live up to what I considered fireable—the person in question had clicked on a phishing message. What if your CEO clicks a phishing message?

In his book *Organizational Culture and Leadership*, Edgar Schein tells the story of Tom Watson Jr., the CEO of IBM between 1956 and 1971.[2] Widely recognized as one of the greatest leaders in IBM's history, Watson created a culture of trust from the top down. When one of his young executives made some bad decisions that cost the company millions, he summoned the executive into his office. When the executive walked in, hat in hand, he said, "After that set of mistakes I suppose you will want to fire me." Watson replied, "Not at all, young man; we have just spent a couple of million dollars educating you." Lots of people get fired for cybersecurity breaches. CIOs. CEOs even. Whether that is a good or bad thing depends greatly on whether we learn any lessons from our education. Watson went on to say, "If you want to double your success rate, double your failure rate."

Don't get me wrong, sometimes getting rid of a problem's source is the right call. Security is a leadership issue, and the business needs to strike the right balance. It's not surprising that, increasingly, leaders are being held accountable for that balance. But firing a CEO, CIO, or CISO assumes the company will change as a result; otherwise, those individuals are just the scapegoats allowing the company to keep the wrong balance.

What if, instead of leading to positive changes, the firing of CEOs had the opposite effect? What if the high-profile firing of executives led to creating cultures in which people didn't want to see potential gaps in security because of what they might find if they went looking? If you don't look for a breach, you don't have to disclose it.

If your policy is to fire after an incident, you need to consider the costs. It may cost human resources upward of $10,000 in recruiting fees to place an average employee, while it may cost upward of $150,000 to place a senior executive. The search could take months, and it could take months to train a replacement, which translates into lost productivity during that time. Would spending $10K or $150K toward security training for the existing employee be a better investment for the company?

What if the company gets hacked again? People like to focus on repeat offenders because there is a pattern of behavior, which surely means they should be punished. I'm not sure it's as simple as that, however. We frequently tell people that it's easy to social engineer someone or that, with a little research, you can craft a phishing email. The repeat offense could be a sign not of ignorance or trainability but that the offender is a more frequent target because of their position. A mature security training program should take this into account.

In my book *No More Magic Wands*, I argued that rather than focusing on punishment, you should focus on incidents providing the opportunity to learn and change. A leader bearing the scars of a security incident will be more focused and aware of the potential issues. Plus they understand the business and how they got where they are, giving them the most potential to come up with solutions.

At the end of the day, I think we all want cybersecurity to improve. I don't think we can adopt the attitude that everyone who doesn't get it should get pushed out of the way. To be successful, we need to include everyone in our efforts. Experience is the greatest teacher, but learning these lessons requires diligence.

Practice makes perfect

In December 1958, *Life* magazine ran a picture of Richard Scheidt on its cover. Scheidt was a firefighter in Chicago, Illinois. In the picture, he is carrying the lifeless body of a ten-year-old boy, John Michael Jajkowski, out of the charred remains of the Our Lady of the Angels School. Out of the sixteen hundred students who attended the Catholic elementary school, ninety-two children and three nuns who were trapped on the second floor of the building died. Some of the children survived by jumping out of the windows, but because the building had a raised basement, it was more like jumping out of the third floor, and many sustained significant injuries. Perhaps the most shocking part of the story is that the elementary school had passed a fire inspection only a few weeks prior. The story sparked a national outrage that would lead to improvements in fire codes and building design.[3] One change would make a much bigger difference than any of the others.

In 2009 a report prepared by the National Fire Protection Association looked at some of the biggest fires over the previous hundred years. In each case, significant improvements had been made to fire codes. But these code improvements were usually limited to the type of building. Our Lady of the Angels in Chicago led to improvements in school fire codes across the country. The Triangle Shirtwaist fire in New York City, where 146 factory workers died in 1911, led to improvements in factories. The Cocoanut Grove fire in Boston in 1942, where 492 concertgoers died, led to improvements in nightclub fire safety. But all of these changes to fire codes, technology, fire alarms, and architecture left out one of the most important elements in fire safety—people. After Our Lady of the Angels, schools all over the country began conducting regular fire drills.

As in many other places, the problem in Chicago was that people didn't know where to go. In an emergency, people panic. Sometimes they shut down and can't move. By conducting regular drills, we teach them how to react in an emergency, so they don't have to think about solving a problem. They can follow their training. In a similar way, cybersecurity drills in the form of simulated phishing or tabletop exercises can greatly enhance the human response to technology-related crises. But care should be taken when it comes to training. We need to understand the effects, both positive and negative, these drills can have. Active shooter drills, for example, may have a negative effect on young people disproportionate to the benefit gained from preparedness.

There's an old story in law enforcement circles that comes from the era of revolvers. During practice, officers would often dump their spent brass cartridges into their hand after shooting a round rather than letting them fall to the floor where other people might slip and fall on them. Officers then took the time to put the brass in their pockets before reloading so they wouldn't have to pick it up again when cleaning up. After real gunfights, officers were found dead with spent brass in their pockets. Did the seconds they lost pocketing their brass cost them their lives?

In his book *On Combat*, Lt. Col. Dave Grossman describes multiple examples where law enforcement trainers have unintentionally created scenarios that incentivize not just good behaviors but bad ones as well. He calls these bad behaviors "training scars."[4] Grossman details another habit where officers, instead of using a dummy gun, used their hands in the shape of a gun. In real-life situations, officers were observed attempting to make an arrest by pointing their fingers when they needed to draw their weapons.

Reflecting on this, I wonder if our corporate cybersecurity training programs might be creating training scars. While the security community is thinking very critically about ways to measure how much we're improving our security, we've got a blind spot when it comes to whether we're creating any unintended consequences in our organizations. In Grossman's law enforcement example above, some tragic and dangerous conditions had to occur before people took a deeper look at how training might be creating just as many bad habits as it was breaking down.

I'm a big proponent of simulated phishing campaigns to help educate users about the dangers of clicking on links. I am a fan because I've seen how effective they are at reducing click-through rates. But when I first launched this campaign, I worked to get buy-in from our executive leadership. Their only concern was whether the campaign would have any unintended consequences. Would such a campaign, for example, mean that employees wouldn't be as responsive to email? Would it change the culture of the organization from being warm and supportive to being cold and suspicious?

Although I have metrics showing how effective a simulated phishing campaign is, the same can't be said of the effect on other habitual changes inside the organization. As far as I've been able to determine, nobody measures culture. I've had many conversations with CISOs about how we can change the culture of our organizations, whether it is even possible, and whether one person can make a difference. But we're only thinking about one dimension of culture when we think about this problem: security.

Widely held as one of the pioneers of quantum mechanics, the German physicist Werner Heisenberg observed in his uncertainty principle that when you look at something, the act of observing it changes what you see. Cybersecurity culture is Heisenberg's uncertainty principle put into practice—just attempting to measure culture will have an impact on it. The thing in question isn't security; it's people, and we need to think of them like the three-dimensional beings they are. If we in the security community were able to measure the overall culture of our organizations—not just from a security perspective—we would stand a much better chance of changing those cultures. Just being aware of behavior might be enough to change it. Just asking the right questions might start the process of change.

A few years ago, I had the opportunity to do some training with police officers at their departmental shooting range. They've incorporated new training techniques to help defeat training scars before they have a chance to form. As a part of their drills, they practice letting their magazines drop to the ground and immediately loading another rather than carefully removing them by hand. This removes the normal etiquette of the shooting range and replaces it with an emphasis on speed and efficiency. They also had a mini drill: When a pistol malfunctions, they are trained to clear the gun immediately rather than freezing or pausing to examine the weapon. Drills now involve maneuvering sideways from target to target or moving toward a target rather than standing stationary. This prevents freezing and emphasizes taking advantage of your environment. Shooting is also done in different positions or stances, incorporating unholstering the weapon at the beginning but progressing so that officers aren't trained to reholster their weapon after every shot. Shooters practice multiple patterns of shots rather than one at a time, so they don't grow accustomed to checking for success after every single shot; this assumes the degree of inaccuracy that should be expected in a messy, real-life scenario. It also avoids tying up ego with missing a single shot; you don't have time to be disappointed in a gunfight.

Whether you're conducting a tabletop exercise with executives or you've hired a social engineer to test your defenses, you're engaged in an opportunity to drill and train your employees. You should be using these opportunities to test and measure their habits, both good and bad. Just like in the law enforcement training example, you can change training scenarios to attempt to exclude bad habits before they begin. You can include diverse training scenarios around the same practice, so training scars don't have a chance to form. And you can have your drills mimic real-life incidents and breaches to prevent practice etiquette from creating muscle memory.

The tabletop exercises that cybersecurity and risk management professionals engage in usually consist of assembling a company's leadership into a room. A moderator will lead this group through a scenario that would be very similar to how the company might experience a data breach or other hacking-related incident. These exercises can be a powerful force for developing the key connections people need to have before working an actual incident together. They also allow employees to gain familiarity with procedures and find issues or gaps with current policies and procedures. If your company has cyber risk insurance, some insurers will help coordinate the exercises because of the positive impact they can have on an organization's cybersecurity.

The problem with tabletop exercises is that they are often limited to company leaders. Usually, this is purely for logistical reasons since getting everyone in a company together all at once is challenging. The choice also engages some strategy; by simulating the exercise with leadership, cybersecurity leaders can highlight weaknesses in the company's defenses or procedures and help build support for improving those weaknesses. But, just like fire safety, these exercises and improvements leave out one of the most important elements of every company—the people. In my program at SMU, I'd rather send employees through an interactive scenario where they can apply and reinforce their knowledge. These scenarios also provide a much more granular idea of how employees would behave in the field, which can further help refine our procedures, processes, and policies while helping us find areas our training needs to reinforce. This approach feeds back into the diligence habit, allowing us to be even more prepared for the next incident.

Be proactive

In the autumn of 1982, a serial killer was frequenting the drugstores and supermarkets of Chicago. He didn't abduct his victims.[5] He didn't shoot them or stab them. He probably didn't even see them die. He was poisoning his victims. Over several weeks, he bought bottles of Tylenol from these stores. He then methodically returned each bottle to the store where he had originally purchased them to conceal his method from police. Inside each bottle were the same capsules of Tylenol, except the killer had added a rat poison or cyanide. Seven victims were killed. A twelve-year-old girl, a family of three, and three other women all died gruesomely as the cyanide ran through their systems. After a few minutes, they would have become dizzy, then started vomiting. Within hours, they would have started having seizures, and eventually, their hearts would have stopped beating.

The killer was never caught.

Police quickly realized that the Tylenol at each of the stores had come from different manufacturers across the country. The only common point was Chicago. Police patrolled the neighborhoods using loudspeakers to warn everyone to immediately stop using Tylenol.

And they did.

Everyone everywhere stopped using Tylenol.

Copycats sprang up all around the country, targeting not just

Tylenol but other brands as well. This was a nightmare for Johnson & Johnson CEO James Burke. While dealing with the tragedy of the deaths, he was also working with law enforcement, developing ways to stop copycats, and trying to save the company. What Burke did was set the standard all other companies are measured against when it comes to handling a disaster—but this only tells part of the story.

At the time, all drugs came in regular bottles. Tamper-proof seals weren't widely used. Johnson & Johnson pioneered new methods, like induction seals or tamper-evident seals. And most pharmaceuticals came in capsules, which users could open to remove or add substances. Johnson & Johnson changed the industry by moving to solid caplets.

Johnson & Johnson forged partnerships with law enforcement and the Food and Drug Administration (FDA) to help track the criminals. This partnership is part of what led Congress to make drug tampering a federal crime. Several of the copycats were prosecuted under this law.

Perhaps the biggest part of Johnson & Johnson's response was the recall. The FBI and the FDA both recommended that the company recall all of the Tylenol in and around the city of Chicago. Instead, Johnson & Johnson recalled all Tylenol, everywhere. In 1982 dollars, this cost Johnson & Johnson $100 million. Adjusting for inflation, in 2018, this would have cost them more than $260 million. Why would Johnson & Johnson do this?

The answer, it turns out, is that the company never considered doing anything else.

Like many companies, Johnson & Johnson has a mission statement, or credo, as it calls it. The credo is four paragraphs long and fits onto one page. It begins, "We believe our first responsibility is to the doctors, nurses, patients, mothers and fathers and all others who use our products and services." This credo has remained unchanged since 1943. Several years before the Chicago poisonings, Burke had met with the senior leaders in his organization to decide whether to keep the credo or get rid of it. At the time, it was thirty-two years old, and people had largely forgotten it. Instead of updating or changing it, they kept every word—and they posted it in every office around the country. They talked to people about it. So, when the decision about what to do came, they didn't have to think.

Johnson & Johnson's market share after the poisonings dropped from 35 percent to 8 percent. But, with their efforts, Tylenol bounced back and gained the highest market share of any over-the-counter pain medicine.

Thinking ahead, practicing, and diligently focusing on its values led Johnson & Johnson to keep and even increase its market share. This diligence made it a leader in its respective industries, but it also did something bigger. The company created a culture. And culture, as we saw in the previous chapter, is one of the single most important factors in preventing incidents from happening in the first place. The situation Johnson & Johnson faced is not unlike that of many companies after a data breach. While the company itself is a kind of victim, it must also send the message to its customers that they are being put first, not last.

Far from being considered in a vacuum, cybersecurity should be considered in larger terms. You can't look at one company acting alone. When something happens in cybersecurity, the whole community reacts, which leads us to the seventh cybersecurity habit—Community.

7

COMMUNITY

Abraham Harold Maslow was a lonely child. He was born in Brooklyn, New York, in 1908 to parents who were uneducated Jewish immigrants from Russia and who had six other children to feed. They knew the best way to lift their children out of poverty was through education. So, they pushed Abraham, the eldest, toward academic success. Hard. He was a gifted student, but anti-Semitic gangs threw rocks, yelled names, and chased him. He spent most of his time hiding out in the library. Books were his best friends.

Abraham soon developed a theory. He realized some needs tended to take precedence over others. If he was thirsty, for example, it didn't matter if he hadn't eaten. A person would die of thirst long before they starved. But this precedence went further. If a person was caught outside in the freezing cold, and someone offered them a choice between a glass of water and a coat, the freezing person would take the coat. A whole litany of needs needed to be met before reaching one's potential as a human being. Abraham Maslow went on to become one of the most famous psychologists of all time, and his theories are as fundamental as those of Freud and Jung.

Maslow created what he called the hierarchy of needs, a school of thought that emerged in the 1950s as a newer, more positive method of thinking about human personality and its potential.[1] His fundamental observation was that humans have categories of needs, and these needs are not arranged randomly but organized sequentially, like a staircase or ladder. Unless you meet the needs on the first step, you can't move on to the next. Most people are familiar with the foundation of Maslow's hierarchy of needs: food, shelter, sleep—known as physical needs. Someone dying of starvation, Maslow explained, is unlikely to be thinking about love, while someone who is drowning will forget about being hungry.

Maslow called the top-tier of this pyramid self-actualization. Maslow described the top-tier as "peak experiences"—moments of great happiness and high performance where someone actualizes their potential. We know we have this potential and want to see it fulfilled. Nothing is as motivating or satisfying as a taste of this potential. This level requires all basic needs to have been met to the degree where a person is liberated to meet their fullest potential.

Before Maslow, psychologists focused almost exclusively on dysfunctional individuals: people with perceived weaknesses or faults that inhibited them from living "normal" lives. Maslow was the first psychologist to study happy, healthy people—from ordinary people to the extraordinary. I would argue that we have been doing the same thing in cybersecurity. We tend to focus on the person who made the mistake that led to a breach rather than those who performed well or discovered and repaired the mistake. By studying successful people, Maslow created a model that people and organizations can follow to unlock their potential. The nine cybersecurity habits embraces the approach of studying successful security leaders to help create a model to follow to be secure, but security itself is also a fundamental need in Maslow's pyramid.

To move up the pyramid to the highest levels of achievement in life, people need more than just meeting their basic physical needs. The second tier as you move up the pyramid is also the most forgotten: safety and security. The first tier of Maslow's pyramid is personal. Assuming they are not ill or infirm, and assuming no other competition, most adults should be able to provide the items on this first tier for themselves. They can hunt for food or grow crops. They can find a cave or build a shelter. They can find water sources and contain water for later use. This isn't true for the second tier. The unique thing about security is that it is, by necessity, a community activity. Security is a collective process. You may be the biggest and strongest caveman in the world, but if you are alone, you might get eaten by a tiger in your sleep or have your possessions stolen by another caveman. The good news is people are hardwired to want to play a role in their own security. We've evolved to be social animals precisely because we need mutual protection. Whenever we come together as a group, this need comes into play.

It is, perhaps, ironic that a lonely boy in Brooklyn would develop a theory for how to build a stronger community. Since security requires a community, one of the natural functions of a group of individuals is providing safety and security—whether this group is a country, a corporation, a church community, or a family. What differentiates good companies or teams from great ones is that the very best help individuals reach their highest potential. This isn't possible if people feel like they will be made into a scapegoat because of an organization's culture of blame. We also fail to reach our potential if a company has such significant security issues that employees fear the inevitability of an incident. In either case, if individuals don't feel safe and secure, they won't reach the top of Maslow's pyramid. Or worse, the entirety of their attention will be consumed after an incident occurs as they try to find some degree of security from another source.

What if our job as leaders isn't to coerce our employees into blindly complying with the policies we write for them but creating experiences where they develop the confidence to set their talents free and pursue their potential? As leaders, our job is proving to our employees how good they already are, how good they can become, and how much capacity they have for being great. The foundation this potential for success is built on is a community of people willing to work together for their mutual protection. This approach requires us to create a culture of cooperation, where it's okay to tell our stories, where we're not shamed for making mistakes, and where we can ask questions if we're not sure what to do. That's the power of a community.

Don't compete—cooperate

President Bill Clinton was responsible for one of the most progressive initiatives in cybersecurity history, helping to increase the security of nearly every industry. In May 1998, President Clinton signed Presidential Decision Directive 63. Now known as Critical Infrastructure Protection, this directive established the concept of information sharing and analysis centers (ISACs). Today, the National Council of ISACs has twenty-five member centers, each representing a different industry sector, such as banking, water and wastewater plants, and higher education.

Companies in each of these industries join an ISAC and share information with one another. For example, the Research and Educational Networks ISAC that universities are a part of has regular in-person meetings, as well as an active email list with hundreds of messages per day sharing information about ongoing attacks, experiences with common vendors, or advice on writing policy for member institutions. This allows each member's security community to mature at a more rapid rate than if it were to go it alone. This community-building process doesn't have to be limited to huge corporations or governments; neighborhood associations and PTAs are formed for the same reasons.

The phrase "loose lips sink ships" comes from a series of propaganda posters created by the US government during World War II. The "loose lips" campaign was meant to remind citizens, government officials, and military officers not to talk openly about the war. The problem with this approach when it comes to cybersecurity is that it values secrecy over community. Most likely, the hackers already have more information about an industry, company, or government than most people are aware of. The only way to combat this imbalance is through communication.

One big issue we face as an industry is that we don't always think of the bad guys as our competition. Instead, we compete with the company down the road who might try to recruit our best people. Vendors think other vendors are their opponents. What if we cooperated instead of competed?

Have you ever heard someone in cybersecurity talk about the bear in the woods? They'll say they don't have to outrun the bear; they just have to outrun you. The bear, in this metaphor, is the hacker trying to break into our networks and steal employee credentials. The idea here is that you can avoid hackers by being a little better than your competitors. This is the scarcity mindset at work, and unfortunately, it's wrong. JP Morgan has more cybersecurity resources than some governments, but it was a victim of hackers. Even the National Security Agency (NSA), arguably home to the greatest minds in security, was hacked. Hackers have many kinds of motivations. Hackers also use automated tools to find weaknesses everywhere.

What would a mentality of abundance in cybersecurity look like? Again, from Stephen Covey's *7 Habits*: "The Abundance Mentality . . . flows out of a deep inner sense of personal worth and security. It is the paradigm that there is plenty out there and enough to spare for everybody. It results in sharing of prestige, of recognition, of profits, of decision-making. It opens possibilities, options, alternatives, and creativity." Abundance requires a sense of security. Because of the threats we face in the field of cybersecurity, whole organizations may have lost their sense of abundance, making our businesses less effective.

Over the past several years, the cybersecurity industry has embraced this concept of community. What started out as few dozen ISACs has exploded into a multitude of regional information sharing and analysis organizations. In 2008, when it looked like corporations were starting to move their servers and services to the cloud, the community came together to form the Cloud Security Alliance (CSA). Today, the CSA offers training, certification, best practices, and policy, but it also creates standards for vendors selling cloud services to make those services more secure. Instead of competing, cybersecurity vendors have started to cooperate.

Security companies collect a lot of intelligence on the activities of malicious actors, much of which is obtained through their customers. If this information is hoarded by just one company or vendor, the community can't learn from that data. Several of the largest cybersecurity vendors in the world came together to form a not-for-profit partnership called the Cyber Threat Alliance to share data with one another. This goes against every competitive practice taught in business schools across the country, but by protecting the community, the members of the alliance respond to a higher calling to secure everyone, not just their customers.

Employ herd immunity

As I raise my child, I'm continually amazed at how fragile we are as a species. What's more, how do animals survive in the wild? Herds of giraffes or antelope must face illnesses and fight off large predators. We're in a similar situation with cybersecurity. Hackers are like predators lying in wait for unsuspecting businesses. How do animals protect themselves from lions, tigers, and bears? They use the power of the herd. Companies, too, can benefit from herd immunity when it comes to security.

In the field of computer science, Metcalfe's law and Reed's law discuss how the value and utility of large networks, particularly social networks, scale exponentially with the number of members. We need exponential improvements in cybersecurity, and herd immunity is how we get there.

From an economic perspective, if enough people and businesses have strong enough security to block certain types of attacks, it makes those types of attacks less effective and, consequently, less profitable to the criminals who perpetrate them. If an attack is less profitable, even companies without strong enough security will have some protection against that attack, since cybercriminals will invest in the most profitable work. The stronger and larger the herd, the greater the protection.

For herd immunity to work, a herd needs to be composed of strong individuals with healthy immune systems. In cybersecurity, this means that, as a country, the stronger our cybersecurity for a larger number of companies, the better off the remaining companies, particularly small businesses with limited resources. This is why information sharing between industry groups is critical.

A healthy immune system has five parts:

- External security
- Internal people and processes
- Communication and intelligence sharing
- Employee training and degree programs
- Internal technology protections

There's a lot at stake for companies when it comes to cybersecurity. Whether we are practitioners, vendors, law enforcement, or business leaders, we have a responsibility to improve our own security for the benefit of the rest of our communities and our country.

"Security has a poverty line," says Wendy Nather, CISO for Duo Security, recently acquired by Cisco Systems.[2] Nather used this phrase at the RSA conference in 2013 after looking at how some large corporations have hundreds or thousands of individuals dedicated to security every day, while most organizations are lucky if they have a single person. But every company, large or small, has many people who hear about cybersecurity challenges and think about what they can do to protect themselves at least part of the time. This collective community effort can be harnessed and used to improve the security of the entire group.

Participation is the key to harnessing this effort. Over time, collective participation and shared stories can be captured and compiled into community resources, further protecting the community.

Create a cybersecurity wellness program

Think about when you go to the doctor's office. What do they do? They look at your pulse, your blood pressure, your weight, and so on. Sometimes they take samples of your blood and run tests on it to check your cholesterol or your white blood cell count. After they've taken quantitative measurements, they move on to qualitative ones. They ask how you feel and listen to your description of your symptoms. They listen closely and ask questions as they narrow down the possibilities of what might be causing your ailment.

We need to do the same thing with cybersecurity. We need to ask questions and make an assessment, though you should realize that there is some danger that the person answering the questions may be just telling us what they expect we want to hear. So, how you present these questions is very important. Keep in mind that your initial assessment is just a baseline measurement, and follow-ups should become routine, like an annual checkup at the doctor's office. And like doctors, you need to be careful about choosing questions that are good indicators of potential problems. Since you can't ask an unlimited number of questions, this is particularly important. You must choose relevant questions that will have value year over year in demonstrating how your security has improved or declined.

We reevaluated our cybersecurity program at Southern Methodist University by adopting this assessment-based approach. We developed a fifty-question survey for all staff and faculty. Our questionnaire asked questions relative to how people used specific technologies, but also helped to baseline our employees' technical abilities and access to sensitive information. The survey provided critical insights on how we would conduct future training efforts. For example, only about one-third of our employees backed up their personal computers, so one of the things we focused on in the following year was the importance of backing up computers.

Most people hadn't considered the importance of saving family photos if their computer hard drive were to break, get destroyed in a fire, or be infected with ransomware. This also helped to dispel some myths we had been telling ourselves about cybersecurity in general. We typically tell people not to use social media because it is dangerous, for example. But analysis of our survey results indicated the opposite. The more a person used social media, the less likely it was for them to have reported being the victim of identity theft. Why? One explanation is that the more a person uses social media, the more likely it is that they have been exposed to the dangers of that service and know how to better protect themselves online. Although perhaps counterintuitive, the implication of this is that, rather than training users to never use social media, we might be better off instructing them to use it more regularly in order to inoculate themselves against common scams or threats.

Most cybersecurity awareness programs fall short of achieving real change because they don't start with an assessment. They don't ask questions to understand the unique conditions and needs of each person. Instead, they treat security education like any other once-a-year mandatory training designed to just check a box in some compliance report. The training is boring. Employees tune out because the information isn't personal to them. Employees don't engage because it's only once per year instead of ongoing. Even the term "awareness" implies that we don't want employees to actually do anything—and that couldn't be further from the truth.

What might an alternative program look like?

As we've explored how habits are formed, we now know it can take anywhere from three weeks to two months to establish a habit. But there is good news. Corporations have realized that healthier employees have lower health-care costs and higher productivity. They've built programs to help change employee behaviors by helping them break out of their old bad habits. They incentivize healthy habits, provide screenings for preventable illnesses, and educate employees about incorporating changes into their lives. They call these efforts wellness programs; most Fortune 500 companies have some variation of a wellness program in place. We can realize the same benefits by incorporating cybersecurity into these programs.

A company could implement a cybersecurity wellness program in a variety of ways. First, the program must fit within your corporate culture. Maybe that means it should be part of your overall wellness program. Your program should be a multiyear plan incorporating incremental steps toward better security and include well-defined goals and outcomes for what can be accomplished. It should start with an assessment of general employee wellness. Have they been the victim of identity theft? Has their Facebook account been compromised? Has the company done a cybersecurity culture audit? Perhaps you can incorporate the results of a simulated phishing exercise or social-engineering test. Next, you need to provide feedback. Most wellness programs offer a customized score that helps users understand what they, individually, may need to work on. Department heads should receive aggregate scores for their areas so they can understand their employee risk profile.

Your education programs can then be custom tailored to meet each employee's needs and prioritized based on the level each employee is at in their training. Some wellness programs offer challenges to help create engagement with the program. Your company can offer webinars or brown bag sessions, whatever is most suited to your culture. Finally, the program should be evaluated. Did the company experience any incidents? How did the program impact that incident? Did the program achieve its defined goals or outcomes? Can you tie back the program to a reduction of insurance premiums or other savings to show a return on your investment? Finally, employees who participate in the program should be recognized in an annual event that refers to learning efforts.

Cybersecurity isn't something you will improve by offering the same thirty-minute course year after year. In a university setting, you start with 101 classes, then progress to 202 and 303. Your cybersecurity program should progress year over year to help build a community of employees who practice good security both at work and at home.

How can we as leaders strive together when it comes to cybersecurity? The simplest way is to have our own philosophy. And perhaps the best place to start our philosophy of being "Well Aware" is to begin thinking of ourselves as coaches instead of czars or the network police. A coach would look at the problem of cybersecurity awareness and say we need to model good behavior to break those bad habits tripping us up. If you asked a coach to name the strongest part of their team, what would they say? The ball? The field? The new technology in the ball? The new cleats they use? The new gloves? The sports drink they use? Or would they say their players?

Aristotle wrote, "Friends hold a mirror up to each other; through that mirror, they can see each other in ways that would not otherwise be accessible to them, and it is this mirroring that helps them improve themselves as people."[3] Mirroring is the way we need to coach one another, and it is the eighth cybersecurity habit.

8

MIRRORING

Dr. Giacomo Rizzolatti was in his lab at the University of Parma, in the northern part of Italy. A professor in the neuroscience department, he was studying the brain of the macaque monkey. He and his team of researchers wired the monkey's head with microelectrodes to watch its brain activity while it performed basic tasks like picking up and eating peanuts. The monkey was strapped into what amounted to a high chair, and its head was fixed looking forward so it couldn't wiggle out of the electrodes. The research team quickly spotted which neuron fired when the monkey performed certain tasks. When the monkey picked up a peanut, neurons fired in a different part of the brain than during the act of eating the peanut. This was interesting but not particularly groundbreaking. So, Rizzolatti did what any good professor would do in this situation: He went to lunch and left a graduate student in charge of the monkey.

Rizzolatti's student also ate lunch, but the student had packed an ice cream cone for his dessert. He ate the dessert in full view of his subject. He still had the monkey strapped into its high chair. As he ate the cone, he noticed something strange; the same part of the monkey's brain that had been triggered when the monkey picked up its food fired when the student picked up the ice cream cone. When he took a bite of the ice cream, the same part of the monkey's brain fired just as it had when it had eaten its own food.[1] This result was so unexpected that when Rizzolatti and his team published the first paper in the mid-1990s, they gave it a name: mirror neurons.

If you've ever watched an athlete get injured and felt a pain in the same part of your body, most likely this is due to your own mirror neurons firing. More recent studies have speculated that mirror neurons serve to help us learn new skills by watching others. In 2005 at UCLA, Dr. Marco Iacoboni decided to take the study of mirror neurons a step further.[2] He placed several human subjects in a functional magnetic resonance imaging machine and played several movie clips of a hand lifting a coffee mug. The movies displayed the hand of a person lifting the mug to drink and a hand lifting the mug to clean up afterward. The images of the subjects' brains suggested the mirror neurons didn't just connect the mechanical action of picking up a cup, they also fired in different ways because the mirror neurons automatically understood the differences in intention between the two different activities. This implies something much greater—that mirror neurons play a role in helping form the social bonds that connect us. To put it another way, our brains are hardwired for empathy. "We are exquisitely social creatures," Rizzolatti said in a 2006 New York Times article. "Our survival depends on understanding the actions, intentions, and emotions of others."[3]

Mirroring today has been loosely defined as a behavior where one person unconsciously mimics another in a number of ways: their gestures, mannerisms, or body language. As it relates to cybersecurity, we use mirroring to see in others those subconscious behaviors that, as Aristotle said, might be otherwise inaccessible to ourselves. But we need not limit ourselves to just looking at our friends for this insight. Most social media accounts allow you to view your profile as though you were an anonymous stranger. We can use Google to search for our names, email addresses, or phone numbers. And we can do the same for our companies or organizations.

Mirroring is also a technique used by salespeople, interviewees, and social engineers to get what they want from others. Salespeople use this technique to quickly establish rapport with their clients, paving the way for a potential deal. One study suggested that candidates who mirror the body language of their interviewer were significantly more likely to be selected for a job. Social engineers use mirroring to blend into the environment they are attempting to infiltrate, making it less likely they will be stopped. But you can also use mirroring to help protect yourself from hackers and transform your organization. Just like how mirror neurons in our bodies play a key role in our social bonds, we need to use mirroring when it comes to the internet to make sure we navigate virtual dangers and maintain our online presence with intentionality by using the other cybersecurity habits we've already learned. Because you can't "see" the cyber world like the real world, it's even more important to build the mirroring habit into your online life.

Perform penetration tests

One Sunday afternoon, Jim Broome sat in a rental car in a parking lot at the back of a nondescript shopping center in Atlanta, Georgia. It was the middle of summer and it was humid. Broome and a colleague stepped out of the car and walked to the back door of the shopping center, carrying several plastic shopping bags from the hardware store across the street. Inside the bags were some power tools and something that looked like a bathroom plunger sticking out of the back. There were cigarette butts strewn on the ground around the back door. Broome had been expecting to have to cut the lock with his power tools, but the door was unlocked, so they walked right in. Apparently, the smokers who worked inside had gotten tired of getting locked out on their smoke breaks.

The inside of the building was cold. It was a data center, and the thousands of servers inside needed to be kept cold because of all the heat they generated. Some of the servers and network equipment inside the building helped run a major internet service provider—and that's what Broome was after. Broome and his coconspirator wore plain-looking polo shirts and badges they had printed a few minutes before at the printing shop just around the corner. The equipment they were interested in was inside a locked cage in the middle of the facility. Broome dumped the shopping bags into a cart stationed down the aisle of metal cages and got to work. It was about 5:00 p.m., when the shifts were changing over from day to night. This meant Broome had a small window to get in and get out before he was caught. The suction cup device came out of the bag and was used to pull up one of the floor tiles, revealing a hollow area under the cage, strewn with wires. Broome's skinny coconspirator dropped down under the floor and popped back up on the other side. He opened the door to the cage. A couple of battery-powered drills came out of the bags, and in a few minutes, the cart was full of servers.

By then, the security team had taken notice of Broome and his companion. As Broome rolled the cart full of servers toward the back door to their rental car, the security guards helpfully held the doors for them. Apparently, the guards thought Broome was supposed to be there to work on the equipment. How else would he have gotten in? There were a lot of servers and network equipment to steal, so it took several trips back and forth to the car. Each time, the car got lower and lower, until the wheels almost touched the frame of the car. On the last trip, the security guard helped them load the final servers into the car.

Broome is the president of the cybersecurity firm DirectDefense, based out of Denver, Colorado, and a penetration tester. The theft of the servers was approved by executives at the company. They gave Broome the green light to do his worst; after all, the company thought they had perfect security and that Broome would get caught at the front door. This specific test took down internet access for hundreds of customers but was just a taste of what a real attacker could have accomplished given significant time, preparation, and motive. The assessment was done with gloves off; Broome had the approval to take any steps necessary to get in, short of threatening or hurting anyone. Most penetration testers today aren't given carte blanche anymore—assessments are usually conducted in more controlled environments, and steps are taken to ensure service to customers isn't affected.

This wasn't Broome's first experience hacking someone to show them their security weaknesses. He did that when he was eleven years old. And the first organization he "helped" was the National Security Agency. It also inspired Broome to start helping companies look at themselves in the mirror when it comes to security. Since then, Broome has helped governments and Fortune 500 companies alike by performing penetration tests. Penetration testing is a way for a company to look at itself from the outside to see where its weaknesses are, just like a person might Google themselves to see what results pop up.

Broome has observed that companies emphasizing this habit of looking at themselves from an outside point of view become more competitive in the market as a result. When smart electric meters were first being tested, one of the top hackers in the world happened to live in that area. The hacker started causing problems for them quickly. It was a lucky break for the company, which began using Broome's team to "pen test" its services to find where the hacker was getting in. Customers recognized the company's leadership in cybersecurity, and consequently, it became a market leader with a six-month head start on the competition. Because the company had built mirroring into its culture, it was able to withstand a nation-state attack against the power grid, while its competitors' products hadn't gone through those same lessons learned.

Looking within

Sarah Hendrickson was almost skipping as she went to a meeting that would change the way she worked with people. While she was on vacation, her boss had found a new technology that would solve one of their biggest security challenges. At the time, Hendrickson was the CISO for a large retail organization and an even larger online shopping portal. The problem was that their customers' accounts were getting compromised—not because the retailer's security had been compromised but because the customers had clicked on phishing messages. Because the customers used the same password on the retailer's website, hackers were going shopping and leaving the customers and the retail giant holding the bag. Usually, websites employ a CAPTCHA, which stands for "completely automated public Turing test to tell computers and humans apart." The retailer didn't want to put these CAPTCHAs in place to help deter bots from using the website for this kind of activity because it would have made the site feel impersonal to customers, and the retailer had a reputation for a very personalized experience. The new technology solved all that—at least it was supposed to.

Walking into the windowless conference room, Hendrickson noticed something was off. The people in the room weren't smiling like she was, and some were several levels above her in the organization. The meeting didn't go well. In solving one problem, the security team had inadvertently created another. When customers go to a retail website, a retailer can usually tell where they are coming from. To effectively market to its customers, the company needed to know when customers were being redirected from Google or an email or were going to the website directly. The security technology the retailer put in place made it look like all of its customers were coming from one device inside its network—the new security appliance.

Hendrickson began her career as a research chemist for a food company. She is tall—six feet, in fact. When she first started there, her boss was short, standing at five foot two. When she and her boss took system measurements, she noticed their numbers were different based on their different perspectives. One of her first assignments was to write some code to calibrate the measurements and eliminate these differences. This understanding of perspective led Hendrickson to work differently with her business stakeholders at the retailer. She fixed the issue with the technology and then went beyond it. She wanted to understand the business. She asked questions. Then, an unexpected thing happened; the business started asking her more questions about how to secure other parts of their organization. This is the unexpected secret to Hendrickson's success: By building a team of partners that valued security, she was able to help the company transform itself after experiencing a breach. Hendrickson's organization held a mirror up to her and her security team, and they looked inside themselves and changed. This self-reflection was infectious.

Tolstoy once wrote, "Everyone thinks of changing the world, but no one thinks of changing himself."[4] Gandhi put it another way: "If we could change ourselves, the tendencies in the world would also change. As a man changes his own nature, so does the attitude of the world change towards him." Tolstoy and Gandhi argue that everyone must change themselves in order to change the world around them. And that perspective change requires each of us, as individuals, to change first. I think this change also requires us to suspend our judgment of others.

Carl Rogers wrote the book on problem children. He pursued a PhD from Columbia after doing research work with troubled children in New York City in the 1920s and 1930s. Rogers later became a professor of clinical psychology, but his early experiences with children shaped his view on how to help people work through their problems. In short, you can't judge people and expect them to change.

His theory became known as "unconditional positive regard." This understanding shapes how every therapist today treats their patients; therapists must set aside their own personal opinions and biases. In Rogers's words, "The individual has within him or herself vast resources for self-understanding, for altering her or his self-concept, attitudes, and self-directed behavior—and that these resources can be tapped if only a definable climate of facilitative psychological attitudes can be provided."[5] This means the therapist must get out of the patient's way so the patient can recover and grow.

In cybersecurity, we judge and assign blame to the adults in our workplaces rather than accepting them for who they are. This judgment prevents us from improving because we're too busy telling other people they should improve. We convince ourselves we're not the ones with the problem. And this can lead to all kinds of trouble. One of the most common reasons people fall victim to social engineering or outright fraud is because they don't believe it can happen to them. If you don't believe it can happen to you, you won't believe that it's necessary to perform a penetration test, Google yourself, view your Facebook profile as though you were a random stranger, or conduct vulnerability scans. If we aim to help individuals and organizations grow and become more secure along the way, then we first need to assess what we need to change about ourselves to facilitate security.

If we were to take Rogers's advice and look at ourselves to change, how would we go about doing it? It can be next to impossible to be objective when it comes to our own actions. When we think about ourselves, it's like looking through rose-colored lenses; according to Rogers, anything threatening to our own worldview is filtered out. On top of that, every time we make a change, a cascade of other changes happen, which must also be reexamined. This is what makes therapy so helpful: You have a neutral party to assist in observing you. But not everyone is in a place where they are comfortable with therapy, and the therapy itself may not be a priority because of other, more basic needs. In a way, the solution is simple. You can pretend to be a different person observing yourself or your actions. Or, to put it a different way, you can learn to see yourself through different lenses. Some lenses may be rose-colored, others might use night vision, while still others could be carnival-mirror-shaped, enlarging and focusing on specific parts of you.

The practice of using lenses requires building empathy. To truly see yourself from another person's perspective requires understanding and validating the other person. Instead of telling this person what you would do in their place, you must consider what that person would do in your place. This also applies to employees needing to understand what the owner of a business would do in a given situation. We use our mirror neurons to have empathy for others. Empathy is what allows us to put ourselves in their shoes and understand how they're feeling. We can also use empathy to go a step further and understand what they would think and feel when they look at us, our behaviors, our data, and so on, and then use this understanding to help eliminate our own cognitive biases.

To improve your mirroring by using lenses, Rogers recommends performing several tasks, listed below. As you review these tasks, think specifically about how you use technology and your data. As you review your social media profiles, perform Google searches, review your credit scores, or even perform penetration tests, consider how others in your organization, your community, or your family would think about each item.

- Set aside your viewpoint and try to see things from the other person's perspective.
- Validate the other person's perspective.
- Examine your own attitude for potential conflicting beliefs.
- Listen for what the other person values.
- Ask what the other person would do.

Avoiding blind spots

Most people who've gone through driver's ed know there's an area behind a car that you can't see in any of your mirrors. Driver's ed courses teach students that you have to turn around and check your blind spot. Despite this, people forget to check their blind spots often enough that some cars now have lights in their mirrors that illuminate when the car senses another car in that spot. Another thing to remember about blind spots is that even good drivers who remember to check their own blind spot don't necessarily realize when they're in someone else's blind spot. When it comes to cybersecurity, how do you know where your blind spots are? How do you know when you're in someone else's blind spot? How can you avoid blind spots altogether?

I recently evaluated two companies regarding their security operations center (SOC) services. Each had some great staff members with years of experience. Each had lots of great technology. Before I went through the process, I wasn't sure which factors would be most important: Would I just go with the cheapest solution, so long as it met my minimum requirements? Would I go with the one that sent the most alerts? Or the one that found the most interesting alerts?

As it turns out, the process of evaluating two different vendors provided a way to find each of their blind spots. Each found alerts the other had missed. For example, one was able to identify sensitive information being transferred on the network when the other wasn't. One vendor was able to identify when a server had stopped sending logs when the other didn't—a server that stops logging could be because of a problem with the server, a power outage, or a hacker stopping logs. Now, it's not necessarily feasible or even responsible to have two different SOCs. But that's how blind spots work—until you look, you won't know. We use this same process to evaluate lots of different technologies, from intrusion prevention to antivirus software. Scientists use this same method to eliminate bias from their research.

Blind spots are part of nature. Even our eyes have them.

Try this experiment. Close your left eye. Look directly at someone's face about ten feet away. Slowly move your eye to the left (toward your nose) about fifteen degrees. At the right distance, the person's face you were admiring will disappear from your vision. This is due to the natural blind spot in your eye that falls in the small circle where your optic nerve attaches to the retina. At that spot, you have no visual receptors, creating a small blind spot in each eye. The effect is subtle; you may not notice unless you're looking for it. Your brain compensates for these blind spots by stitching together the images from each eye to fill in the two blind spots and create one complete image. The perspective of one eye alone is incomplete. You need the added perspective of the other eye to see the whole picture.

Your mind has evolved to fill in the blind spot with the textures or colors of what is around the blind spot because it assumes there is very little chance something important is there.

Daniel Kahneman, the Nobel Prize-winning psychologist who created the field of behavioral economics and the theory of cognitive bias, writes that, essentially, brains are lazy. Our minds tend toward the least amount of thinking required for any task. This results in what he calls the phenomena of "what you see is all there is."[6] Because our brains have been designed to minimize cognitive load, they don't look for the most complete picture before making a decision because we believe we already see the whole picture. Because you can't see your data or the internet, this makes it even more challenging to keep your brain engaged in the process of looking for vulnerabilities. The habit of mirroring is what can have the biggest impact on overcoming our own limitations.

One blind spot the cybersecurity industry has is diversity.

Several years ago, I posted a job opening for a senior security engineer position on my team. This position required years of experience; the new employee would be the lead technical security person on my team. Frequently, the cybersecurity job market has been described as having negative unemployment, which means there are more job openings than people to fill those jobs. This has led to drastically increased salaries for the jobs that are open, and not all the candidates looking to change jobs are necessarily qualified to fill them. When I began interviewing candidates, I found out the truth of this situation. I only got a handful of responses. Of the ones that applied, one was a bodybuilder with part-time security experience as a security guard. When we conducted interviews, one of the more experienced candidates dropped an "F-bomb" in the interview. After several months, we used an external recruiter who was able to place us with a great candidate, but the position had gone unfilled for over six months, which meant the team wasn't making as much progress as we needed to.

When two more job openings came up a year later, I decided to reexamine the process. What I learned changed the way I hire employees. As a university, one of the biggest benefits we offer is a discount on tuition, so I got rid of the college degree requirement. For the same reason, I also got rid of the industry certifications requirement. I wanted to recruit people in the middle of their careers, with years of experience, but whose employers weren't able to provide the time or funding for them to complete a degree or obtain certifications. Unsurprisingly, I received a lot more résumés. And the number of female applicants also dramatically increased. Ultimately, the two candidates I hired were both women, which made my team unusual since only about 20 percent of the workforce is female in cybersecurity.

I later learned that my change in the hiring process aligned with the advice human resources experts give companies that want to make a difference when it comes to gender diversity. Studies have shown that when women see a job description with ten qualifications of which they only meet nine, they won't apply. When men see a job description with ten qualifications, and they only have three, they apply anyway. The answer isn't necessarily to reduce your qualifications as I did. Human resources experts also recommend stating clearly that if you don't meet all of the qualifications but are passionately interested in the job or the company, you are still encouraged to apply.

Having a team composed of 50 percent women has made me aware of my own blind spots—not just in recruiting but in how I manage the team and how I interact with the rest of my organization. If your company is 50 percent women, but your security team is 80 percent men, chances are you won't be adequately representing the needs of the company. This is true not just in technology but for all areas of organizations that are traditionally male dominated. Women bring a different perspective to projects and meetings. The women I work with can read a room and people's reactions differently than I can, and this is a very healthy thing for both my team and the entire organization. Diversity helps our team eliminate error and cognitive bias while providing better feedback and advice to the company.

From a security perspective, what pushes us to look for things that might be in our blind spots? As Kahneman says, our brains are lazy, and we might not be looking. For many businesses, this act of looking may come with a disincentive. If you discover something, you might have to fix it, and perhaps the resources aren't there to do so. Worse, if you discover something, someone might get fired because they weren't doing their job. Diversity is a part of making everyone feel included, but it allows you to prevent groupthink, eliminating the blind spots you would have had otherwise. And intentionally making room for diversity means that it's safe for others to do the same self-reflection.

Give yourself a makeover

I'm ashamed to admit that I watch reality TV—but probably not the shows you might expect. I'm a big fan of the show *What Not to Wear*. Contestants on the show are nominated by their friends and family, who see someone in desperate need of not just a makeover but a total style upgrade. These nominators even share video of their friend or family member as proof of how clueless they are when it comes to fashion. To go on the show, the people getting the makeover subject themselves to a humbling process. First, they get direct feedback from the two hosts of the show about their current wardrobe. The most grueling aspect is when they try on the worst example of style in their closet and stand in front of a three-way mirror, where the hosts critique them, literally telling them what their look conveys to other people. At the end of this process, the participant must throw away all of the most hideous parts of their wardrobe. It's not all bad, however. The next step is a chaperoned shopping spree. The hosts are charged with finding clothing that matches the person's job, body type, or other unique issues. Stylists help the person learn how to style their hair and makeup to fit their new look. Finally, the person unveils their new look at a cathartic gathering of the same family and friends that outed them as being a style reject in the first place.

I think a cybersecurity makeover should follow a similar process. This process should begin with feedback and a hard look in the mirror. You need an accurate assessment of where you are currently to know where you need improving. Like in *What Not to Wear*, this is the most difficult part of the process because getting honest criticism from our friends, coworkers, and family can be difficult and humbling. One of the most popular ways of assessing yourself today is 360-degree feedback.

The challenge with coaching and developing employees, or with coaching in general, is that the feedback the individual gets is subjective. If a boss or mentor provides feedback, they aren't necessarily seeing the whole picture of the employee's interactions with others. By incorporating feedback from everyone around you, you are much more likely to get an objective assessment that will help you grow and change.

One of the pioneers of this type of feedback is Dr. Marshall Goldsmith. His books have appeared on the *New York Times* and *Wall Street Journal* best-seller lists, and he has been recognized as the number one executive coach in the world. His book *What Got You Here Won't Get You There* is recognized as one of the premier works on how to transform your career. The first thing Goldsmith wants you to do is to learn to observe how other people look at you. You don't have to wait for an annual review to get 360-degree feedback.[7] In *What Got You Here*, Goldsmith offers five rules for observing others, which he describes as observational feedback:

1. **Make a list of people's casual remarks about you.** Make a journal of the interactions you have with people for twenty-four hours. At the end of the day, for each remark, rate the interaction as positive or negative. Did they say "great idea" or "you're late"? Over time, patterns may emerge that will help you shift your behaviors.

2. **Turn the sound off.** In meetings, pretend you are watching a silent film and watch the body language of the people around you instead. Are they bored or listening intently? Or are they ignoring you?

3. **Complete the sentence.** Pick one thing you want to excel at and analyze your motivations by writing down why you want to do that thing. Repeatedly asking the question "Why?" can break through your defenses until you've reached your true motive.

4. **Listen to your self-aggrandizing remarks.** Braggadocian remarks or humble-bragging provide detailed clues about how you see yourself, even if what you say is self-deprecating.

5. **Look homeward.** Many successful individuals aren't necessarily motivated by success or money; they are motivated by family. People want to change because they want to be better husbands and wives, better fathers and mothers. Often, the feedback from this group can make the biggest difference.

Goldsmith offers this advice in the context of management and leadership, but the same feedback loop can be used in the context of cybersecurity. If you observe people expressing concerns about security, you may have an underlying problem. If you listen to remarks about security, are they boastful, like "we can never be hacked," or are they self-deprecating, like "we've probably already been hacked"? Both kinds of comments reveal important aspects of your culture and can be used as guideposts for improvement. Understand why cybersecurity is important to you or your company and use this "why" to help build a shared mission around improving.

Another great way to ensure a proper assessment is by journaling. Journaling can have a dramatic impact on your view of the world. Cybersecurity incidents can be a highly emotional experience, involving stress, fear, and regret. But security can also create positive feelings, like satisfaction at protecting your community and confidence you can have an impact. Writing about and reflecting on these experiences over time can create a trajectory of meaning running throughout your life. Writing down your thoughts effectively doubles the impact of those experiences because it forces you to relive them.

Writing things down also reinforces the good habits you will build along the way. Expressive writing has been shown to strengthen the social connections between people in nearly every context. Writing about emotional experiences has been shown to have several positive outcomes, such as fewer doctor visits, better grades, and better relationships. In one study, researchers found that couples who journaled three days a week for about twenty minutes per session were 50 percent more likely to be dating at the end of three months than the control group of couples who were asked not to journal during the same three-month period.

Think about an experience you had concerning cybersecurity in the past twenty-four hours. Did you have to change your password? Did you use your credit card online or in person? Did you accidentally leave your phone unattended in a meeting or at a shop? Did you visit a website where your browser gave you a warning that it might not be safe? Did you use an insecure wireless access point at your favorite coffee shop or hotel? Did you install a new app on your smartphone that prompted you for permissions you didn't expect to give? For ten minutes, write down every detail you can remember about your experiences over the previous day as they relate to security. If you had a bad experience, think about what made that situation challenging? Is there something that can be done to make it better next time? When you have a great experience, you should also share it with someone else. Sharing spreads the message while doubling the impact because you relive the positive message you learned.

Now that you've analyzed your own environment, it's time to give yourself a cybersecurity makeover. What patterns start to emerge? What baggage do you have to get rid of? This could be in the form of legacy software or out-of-date devices that can't be patched. It could be digital litter taking up room on your computer that needs to be deleted.

You don't need to go on a shopping spree to change out your cybersecurity wardrobe. Starting with the inventory that we built in Chapter 1, think about where your data is and how one of the members of your community from Chapter 7 might view that. Think of how a competitor or a client might view your inventory. If you were starting your business over from scratch, would you treat the data the same? Or would you make different choices? You might not be in a position today to change everything, but the things that you can change, like in a makeover, can be changed dramatically. Larry Page, the former CEO of Google, argues that the services the company builds should be ten times better than the services it currently offers. Often, these "moonshot" ideas are not held back by prior assumptions or requirements. Page believes the chances of a moonshot idea being a wild success increase dramatically precisely because they don't have existing baggage to carry.

Many large organizations employ teams of cybersecurity professionals. Unfortunately, these teams are usually locked away, focused on managing their technology or keeping detailed spreadsheets to prove their compliance with some framework or regulatory rules. Small companies may be lucky to have a few generalist IT employees; most don't have dedicated cybersecurity specialists. What both kinds of organizations need are cybersecurity consultants that can act like the style consultants in our makeover analogy.

In *The Phoenix Project*, author Gene Kim argues that, as companies adopt a DevOps approach, the most effective way of providing security is to embed security specialists to act as consultants in every project. Some companies will have dedicated cybersecurity liaisons dedicated to individual departments. Smaller companies with fewer resources should seek out cybersecurity professionals in their community.

Utilize a bug bounty program

In 1980 James Ready and Colin Hunter started a software company. Today, their Versatile Real-Time Executive operating system powers the Hubble Space Telescope, among other things. But what sets their company apart is their use of mirroring to make over their product. To improve their product, Ready and Hunter ran an ad in the newspaper. If anyone could find a bug in their operating system, they would buy them a Volkswagen Bug. Just like the penetration test, a bug bounty program creates a mirror. Instead of using just one company for the service, you use thousands of individuals, all with unique skillsets, to help you find potential problems before they become actual problems.

Today, companies like Facebook and Google have bug bounty programs designed to proactively find vulnerabilities in their software and patch them before they fall into the wrong hands. These vulnerabilities can be extremely valuable, sometimes offered for hundreds of thousands of dollars on the black market. These bug bounty programs offer companies a way to mirror themselves while also providing incentives for people to find issues and report them to the company rather than a competitor or government that might want to use the bug against them. These incentives are extremely important and are the culmination of the makeover process. People get excited about makeovers for many different reasons. Perhaps they are excited by the prospect of going on a shopping spree, or they're looking for a style change, or they want the validation of having an expert help them. The ultimate reason for a makeover is the transformation, not the incentives along the way.

Cybersecurity successes should be celebrated. This could mean giving incentives to employees for meeting their security objectives for the year, or it could mean paying bounties for finding vulnerabilities. It could mean having an annual awards banquet where you recognize and reward individuals who contributed to improving cybersecurity in meaningful ways. However you celebrate this success, it should be something memorable. Make it something people will talk about all year long so these incentives reinforce the message that cybersecurity is a valuable part of the organization's mission.

There is a technique for making yourself completely cybersecure. You can unplug your computer from the wall, lock all your doors, and weld the windows shut. This isn't good advice, precisely because we are all members of a larger community. We need one another to live full lives. As you participate in a community, you need to practice mirroring both for yourself and for the communities you are a part of. You'll need to understand what information you may be inadvertently leaking and, through mirroring, change it. You'll play a role in helping your community see itself and improve as well. Ultimately, however, not every leak can be patched. Some doors must stay open for good reasons. The previous habits discussed in this book have shown you how to protect those open doors. We should expect, however, that some small fraction of the people that walk through those open doors will come with knowledge, the ability to evade our defenses, and the intent to do harm. This leads to the final and perhaps most controversial habit: deception. Many mature cybersecurity programs today use different forms of deception, but there are examples of deception throughout history. In his *Art of War*, Sun Tzu wrote, "All warfare is based on deception. Hence, when we are able to attack, we must seem unable; when using our forces, we must appear inactive; when we are near, we must make the enemy believe we are far away; when far away, we must make him believe we are near."

Deception is the final habit because it is so difficult to master without altering the culture of an organization.

9

DECEPTION

In the 1980s, Dr. Clifford Stoll was a curly-haired astronomer living in Berkeley, California. He was helping to design the telescope optics that would eventually be used in the Keck Observatory in Hawaii, but then his research grant ran out. Without funding, he needed a job. Luckily, one awaited him in the basement of the building where he already worked: the computer lab. The Keck Observatory was the first telescope designed with smaller hexagonal mirrors to create one large telescope. To coordinate all of those mirrors required sophisticated computers and computer programming, so it was natural for Stoll to move to the computer center downstairs.

On Stoll's first day, he was assigned a much more difficult task: find out why the computer lab's accounting system showed a $0.75 error in the monthly report. The other lab technicians thought it was probably a rounding error or a problem with one of the many accounting programs that had been written by long-gone former student interns. There was no documentation concerning how any of the software worked or how the various programs worked together. Stoll spent hours, then days, then weeks tracking down the source of the problem until he found it.

The culprit wasn't a rounding error or a problem with the software. It was a German hacker working for the Russian government. Stoll worked extensively with the FBI, CIA, NSA, and Air Force to track down the hacker. This is possibly the first example of a computer hacking case ever documented, and Stoll kept an exceptional level of detail in his logs. In 1989 Stoll wrote a book about his experience, called *The Cuckoo's Egg*.

Keep in mind, this happened during the Cold War, the Berlin Wall was still intact, and computer hacking was still very rare. Moreover, no one had ever tracked a hacker before, so no one knew how to do it.

Stoll kept a daily logbook of all of the attacker's activities and the steps Stoll used to monitor him, using the same attention to detail he'd honed as an astronomer tracking stars and comets. From that point onward, his attention to detail became a roadmap for computer forensics, law enforcement, and security experts. Stoll also had a secret weapon. He created what is widely considered to be the first honeypot. To most people, a honeypot would conjure the image of Winnie the Pooh waddling around his home, occasionally getting his head stuck in an earthenware container with sweet yellow nectar spilling out over the edges. In computer terms, a honeypot is an attractive but fake account or network used to flush out hackers. Stoll set up an imaginary department within the Lawrence Berkeley National Laboratory called SDI, populated it with extra computers he had scavenged, staffed it with fictitious people, and created lots of fake documents on the computers for the hacker to find. This allowed Stoll and law enforcement to track the hacker back to his home in Hanover, Germany, ultimately leading to the hacker's arrest.

Along the way, Stoll inspired a generation of cybersecurity professionals. His honeypot formed the foundation for much of what modern cybersecurity professionals take for granted. This allowed him to understand who his adversary was and what he was doing. Perhaps more importantly, it allowed Stoll to understand how the bad guy was doing it. Had Stoll not spent many nights in his sleeping bag inside a data center waiting for the hacker to dial in, we might not have developed these kinds of technologies or forensic practices until much later—and many more companies could have been compromised.

A decade later, in 1998, Lance Spitzner sat in his office, watching his computers being hacked. He lived in Chicago, and his home research lab had seven computers in it, all running different operating systems. Lance is the founder of the Honeynet Project, which has collected reconnaissance data from computers all over the world to help researchers learn hacking techniques from the hackers themselves by setting up a kind of laboratory of real systems to observe the hackers in their element. At the time, most honeypot technologies were just detection-based, and they would create alerts. Lance took it a step further, creating whole networks of real computers the bad guys could interact with so he could monitor their keystrokes, logs, and the tools that were installed or modified. Lance was deceiving the hackers to learn more about them: what their techniques were, what they were after, and where they were coming from.

He used real software behind a real firewall. Lance got old, recycled computers and put them in his office. He then compiled all of the activity into a story about how the hackers were operating. Lance worked with the other members of the Honeynet Project to publish a series of papers called *Know Thy Enemy*; as antivirus companies like McAfee and Symantec raced to keep malware out of the millions of newly internet-connected computers in the early 2000s, the *Know Thy Enemy* papers proved invaluable.[1]

The same individuals Lance observed were caught hacking computers all over the world. With his team at the Honeynet Project, he found individuals who were interested in hacktivism. They found the first automated networks of organized cybercriminals stealing credit cards out of Eastern Europe and watched in real time as criminals typed commands. They also saw the progression toward more automated techniques, including using malware to infect computers. At the height of the Honeynet Project, forty to fifty people from all over the world were involved, each with their own networks of honeypot computers.

The problem with deception isn't that it doesn't work. It works well, especially with the latest advances in virtualization, cloud, and artificial intelligence. The problem is that people don't like being deceitful. At first, the FBI wasn't really interested in working with Stoll because the crime didn't involve much money—remember this started with a loss of $0.75 for the university. Adjusted for inflation, in 2018 dollars this would be $1.60. Money aside, the FBI didn't want to spend the resources on setting up a sting when no one knew if any laws were being broken. People sometimes have misconceptions about deception, such as it being time-consuming or only for organizations with highly mature security programs. However, with the latest technical advances, deception is proving to be highly effective, especially for simplifying detection, threat hunting, and intelligence gathering.

Today, honeypot technologies have been developed that allow companies to set up deception-based networks automatically and that aren't limited to just creating virtual computers. They can create fake accounts that no one should log in to and create fake tokens or virtual customer sessions that no one should be able to access. Many honeypot technologies are detective in nature, meaning they act like a tripwire to find out when someone has gone where they shouldn't and set off alarm bells. But they can be used for other reasons. Attivo Networks, Illusive Networks, and TrapX Security are great starting points.

Modern deception technologies allow security teams to create and recreate whole deception networks in real time. They can extend to the cloud, where security teams lack visibility. They can be used to help visualize an attacker's path into the network and provide greater insights into their capabilities or motives. And they can lure attackers away from where the important data really is. But they can also go too far, alienating users.

I've learned the hard way using simulated phishing campaigns on my campus. It's easy to create a fake email that looks like a legitimate business email. While it's true that hackers don't have to follow rules, security teams need to ensure they don't go too far when "tricking" their users. We always send an email a week or two in advance of a campaign to give people a heads-up. As security practitioners, we need our users to trust us. Ultimately, using deception should create more trust in the business, not less.

Use deception as defense

Umesh Yerram was sitting in his office as the sun was starting to go down on a Friday evening, not knowing how late he would have to work that night. Yerram has been a cybersecurity leader for more than a decade in multiple industries. At the time, he was listening in to a conference call his team of security engineers had put together for a large-scale penetration test. The company's security operations center was buzzing with activity, but Yerram didn't want to distract the team by being in the middle of the action.

The company wasn't under attack from an outside force. Yerram's other team, a group of highly skilled penetration testers, his "red team," was using an attack simulation tool that would mimic how a highly skilled group of attackers might attempt to hack the company. They wanted to see what, if anything, a motivated attacker could get and how their team would respond. Yerram's heart sank when he heard the initial report that the red team had stolen some company credentials. After a few moments, the defenders, known as the blue team, responded that this was part of the plan. The credentials that the red team had stolen were the breadcrumbs that the blue team had left lying around on purpose so that if they were used, that would send an alert that hackers were attempting to compromise a system.

Yerram's strategy early on was to get ahead of the curve by being predictive. Focusing on predictive capabilities has given the companies he's worked for the ability to protect against not just the threats it knows about but the unknown ones as well. "If your strategy and your vision does not include deception as one of the key controls to protect your business," Yerram said, "then you aren't adding value to your security posture." While cybersecurity teams collect all of their data in a centralized logging system, and they've got teams and tools that go through their data, they spend a lot of time chasing down false positives or hunting needles in haystacks. Deception flips this paradigm on its head. Deception allows Yerram's team to focus on high-fidelity alerts for activity that shouldn't have happened in the first place. If someone is going where they shouldn't and rings some bells by touching a breadcrumb or by accessing a decoy network, engineers get a heads-up that a potential bad guy is on their network before they've stolen the crown jewels.

Yerram's team is getting as much if not more out of the deception-based alarms than they get out of the traditional approach of monitoring their server or endpoint logs. His team wants to make it as difficult as possible for an attacker to leave the network. If someone does get past their initial defenses, Yerram wants to know about it, but he also wants to waste the hacker's time while they're inside, which is time they can't spend doing other nefarious things.

But deception doesn't have to be limited to large corporations using cutting-edge technology.

When Elaine met Steve at a party, she was instantly repulsed. When he began talking to her, she preempted all the small talk by giving him a fake number. Elaine had been using the same fake phone number for the past five years, and when she finally called the number, she learned it was the number for a betting parlor. They had been receiving calls from her unlucky suitors for years. While this may or may not be a common occurrence at bars and parties throughout the world, this case is from the opening scene of "The Strike," an episode from the ninth season of the television show *Seinfeld*.

Giving out a fake phone number in 2019 is different from giving out a fake number in 1997. Often, the other party will call the number immediately to save the number in their history rather than creating a new contact. Giving out a fake number is really an attempt to avoid the awkward conversation around rejection—for the person doing the rejecting as well as for the person being rejected. No one wants to be on either side of that equation.

The good news is there's an app for that.

Rather than giving out a fake number, you can now give out a burner number. Burner phones are a staple of spy movies, but you don't need a second phone to have a burner. Apps like Burner, SmartLine, Unlisted, or Hushed can provide a temporary telephone number that routes calls back to your primary phone. Burner numbers can be an important thing for protection, particularly if you are using online dating or to help stop harassment and stalking. Just press a button and you stop getting calls from the burner number.

While these apps help people use deception for privacy, others take it a step further. The company RoboKiller offers an app that stops telemarketers from calling you. In addition to protecting your privacy, RoboKiller increases the cost of doing business for spammers. The app recognizes a spam phone caller and forwards the calls from the spammer to an automated voice system that plays simulated messages back to the telemarketer to keep them on the phone. This ties up the spammer's phone lines and prevents them from calling other people. By keeping the telemarketer talking to what they think is a real person, the cost of the phone call goes up as well.

Deception isn't just a modern phenomenon; it's the oldest trick in the book. And the technology used in deception doesn't have to be limited to computers. The Trojan horse was one of the greatest deceptions in the history of the world. The Trojan War is believed to have happened sometime between 1260 and 1180 BC. The war had gone on for ten years and was essentially a stalemate, with neither side being able to gain a significant advantage over the other. This was a long time, given that the average Greek lifespan at the time is estimated to have been about thirty-five years. So, the warriors on both sides would have spent most of their adult lives on the battlefield. Though many would have wanted to go home and live out the rest of their lives, there was a bit of pride involved in having already spent ten years fighting. The Greeks didn't want to lose face and walk away empty-handed. And so, the Greeks employed deception to bypass the Trojan defenses entirely by building the Trojan horse.

By contrast, if the Trojans had invented the honeypot, they might have built a small version of their city inside the city walls. A waiting room, or lobby, if you will. They could have brought the Trojan horse inside their mini-city and let it sit for a few days. If no Greeks came pouring out of it by the end of the week, then it might be safe to bring the horse inside their walls. If the Greeks did jump out, they'd be trapped inside the mini-city and could be eradicated. What I've described thus far is how some security software protects you from malware. The malware is "detonated" inside a contained virtual computer, and the clock is sped up to see whether the software tries to do anything malicious within a given timeframe.

The Trojan horse, while built by a master carpenter, was constructed in just three days from timber harvested nearby. Today, you don't need to be a computer engineer with a master's degree to use deception. Fake phone numbers or apps are all inexpensive, no-cost solutions for protecting your privacy. Many other simple solutions exist to help prevent you from being a victim online, such as one-time-use credit card numbers, fake answers to password challenge questions to prevent people from guessing your answers and locking you out of your accounts, and different usernames and passwords for administrator accounts on servers or databases. Far from being overly complex or a large commitment, these steps all use a small deception to provide multiple layers of protection that, when combined, are difficult to overcome.

Be prepared

During the 1980s, the Rural Telephone Service Company, a small-town telephone cooperative, provided service to about four thousand customers in northwest Kansas. One of those services was sending phonebooks to these customers. All phone companies are required to provide phonebooks. Sometimes, larger phonebook-producing companies compile telephone numbers and sell advertising throughout a larger area. Feist Publications was one of those companies. It offered to license the customer list from Rural, but Rural refused, the lone holdout from among eleven districts. So, Feist decided to copy all of the information from Rural's phonebook and publish it anyway, without a license. But Rural had set a trap. Rural knew instantly that Feist had copied its information. It had included several fake names and addresses in the phonebook as a mechanism for detecting any theft of its directory. This process is known as watermarking.

Rural put in a detective control that used deception to spot other companies using its information without permission. This became a hotly contested copyright case that went all the way to the United States Supreme Court. Rural won at the trial and appellate court levels but ultimately lost its copyright claim. The Supreme Court ruled that phonebooks aren't copyrightable because they lack the creative spark copyright requires.[2] This was both a win and a loss for Feist. It had won the suit, but the costly victory meant others could copy its phonebooks without licensing from the company.

The truth is a set of one; lies are infinite. If a hacker is looking at your network or making phone calls to your employees to perform reconnaissance, they must assume you are telling the truth when they ask a question. Only you or someone that knows you will know you are lying. These small deceits cost an attacker time. Any conflicting information they receive will frustrate them. Even if they successfully collect some valid information, they can't trust it because they'll have no way of knowing what information is valid and what is bogus.

I saw this play out with an admin assistant I knew. She often answered calls from salespeople looking for her boss, Chris. "He's expecting my call . . ." they would say. Except Chris was a female executive. The assistant would let the salesperson talk, giving them a small cue that could allow them to either correct or dig further into the lie. The callers said all kinds of things about how they knew Chris from college or had dinner the other night, hoping to put the assistant at ease. It didn't matter; the assistant took a message, and the callers wouldn't get through. Eventually, they stopped calling. This process of offering small clues that lead the subject away from their intended target is referred to as dropping breadcrumbs.

Deception requires preparation.

Every actor, public speaker, musician, and preacher rehearses before going in front of an audience. I've given speeches to audiences across the country, and my speech coach recommended I spend six to eight hours before every talk rehearsing the speech before I give it. This is after I've spent hours writing the speech and preparing the presentation. To give you a better idea of how the preparation process works as it relates to deception, I've created the following case study. Keep in mind, we are only talking about using deception to protect yourself or your organization, not to harm others.

I'd like to ask you to make up a TV show. You'll prepare to tell someone else about this TV show as though you've just started watching it and you're excited to tell the other person about it. You'll need to give it a name, talk about what it's about, and say which actors are in it. You should think of three interesting scenarios that happened in the show and be able to recall them if the person is interested and wants to hear more.

Look for the cues in the other person that would indicate to you whether they believe you. Can you tell if they are skeptical? How would you change your story based on something that triggered a response in them? (And if you start feeling guilty after all of this, you may disclose that you were doing an assignment in this book you were reading.) Record your results. How many people were you able to convince? How many were able to see through your story or were otherwise skeptical? What were the red flags that caused them to question your veracity?

Now, let's imagine the reverse scenario. The next time someone is telling you about a TV show they have watched, pretend they are lying—that maybe they haven't watched the show or the show doesn't actually exist. Assume they have done the same preparation that you did: Maybe they read a Wikipedia summary of the episode or are making it up. What questions would you ask them, knowing they've done some preparation already? Can you shoot a hole in the story? Perhaps an actor name they can't remember? Is there a question you can ask them to confirm definitively whether they watched the show? Now, picturing yourself at your own office, what if you assumed someone calling you on the phone or sending you an email was lying? Remember that a social engineer who calls you on the phone will have done this same preparation, or they will have done this kind of thing frequently enough to ad lib very convincingly. What questions would you ask to ensure they were telling the truth?

You might create "lies" you use for common password challenge questions. Or you might set up a honeypot on your internal network to alert you if anyone accesses it. Deception can be both a preventive control as well as a detective one. The strategy I've outlined above will help identify fraud through careful use of traps. Con artists and social engineers carefully research their targets. If you're the target, you must be prepared to tell a convincing lie. You must have a backstory that can stand up to examination because you expect to be challenged. In cybersecurity, we always expect our defenses to be challenged, so we employ some level of deception either to prevent those challenges from succeeding or detect them when they occur.

The habit of deception is, perhaps, the most difficult of the nine cybersecurity habits. Some of the most mature cybersecurity programs implement this habit successfully, and you will be able to do it for yourself just as easily. First, you need to plan one small act of deception and be prepared to use it. That way, you'll be ready when you need to access your fake password challenge question. Some examples of specific cybersecurity deception activities include the following:

- Setting up fake accounts that no one has access to

- Monitoring those accounts for activity and tracking where any login attempts come from

- Lying when creating password challenge question responses so no one can guess the correct answers

- Using "trick" questions to help discover imposters
- Divulging false information on purpose to find leaks

Perhaps the best example of preparation is the greatest deceiver of all time: the magician. Some magicians spend weeks or even months practicing and perfecting a trick before they perform it. By then, the motions of the trick are so natural it looks like they're doing it for the first time.

Ehrich Weiss was stripped naked, chained, and locked in a cell in Germany. Imagine the officer's surprise when Ehrich walked out of the cell, asking for his clothes back. You may know Ehrich by his nickname, Harry—Harry Houdini.[3] During his tour in 1900, Houdini's escape baffled police from Scotland Yard to Russia. Instead of just performing at theaters to large audiences, he gained notoriety by making spectacular escapes from prison cells—or, in one case, a prison transport van—which got the attention of local newspapers. One police officer was so baffled, he alleged Houdini had simply bribed other officers to give him the keys. Houdini sued the officer and won. The case was settled when the judge challenged Houdini to open the safe located in the judge's office, which Houdini did instantly, as if by magic. Houdini admitted later that the judge had neglected to lock the safe. Nevertheless, Houdini's reputation as an escape artist was cemented.

Houdini's father lost his job when Houdini was eight years old, leading the boy to take his first job as a trapeze artist at age nine. At sixteen, he took on the stage name Houdini after reading his first book on magic, written by the French magician Jean-Eugène Robert-Houdin. Houdini began his professional career as a magician only a year later. His initial focus was on card tricks, but many magicians said his sleight-of-hand technique lacked the finesse of other performers of the time. Instead, Houdini found his success at another kind of deception—escapes.

Had Houdini simply broken out of his chains in seconds, most likely he would not be revered as the greatest magician of all time. He might have been a good lockpicker or safecracker because of his skill, but those skills don't necessarily involve deception. Essentially, Houdini was telling a story. His stories were designed to build suspense, but they also allowed him to draw the attention of the audience away from where the real work was going on. For example, in 1904, Houdini was invited to London to break out of a special pair of handcuffs an English locksmith had taken five years to create. The key to the handcuffs was purported to be six inches in length, making it impossible to conceal. The escape dragged on for well over an hour, with Houdini giving the appearance he had been beaten—until, at last, he emerged without the handcuffs. In terms of neuroscience, the audience's stress response increased because they believed Houdini wouldn't escape or that he could. The mirror neurons discussed in Chapter 8 were going crazy, which, in turn, short-circuited any vigilance or skepticism habits the viewer might have employed to logically figure out the trick. In other words, deception hijacks the brain using emotion.

Practicing a handful of deceptive techniques like decoys, breadcrumbs, or watermarking can help you protect yourself and your communities when no other security habit can. This explains why police selectively leak clues to the press to identify imposters. Deception can be an important tool in your arsenal of cybersecurity habits, but it should be used with caution and should only be used as a supplement to all of the other habits. Deception is not a replacement for the other habits; it complements them. Deception helps you know your adversary and allows you, assuming you've mastered all nine cybersecurity habits, to engage them on terrain where you have the advantage.

CONCLUSION

When she was nineteen months old, Helen Keller got sick. She was so sick she lost her vision and her hearing. In the 1880s, there wasn't much hope for children who were both deaf and blind. The world was extremely dangerous for a toddler, and life on a farm was challenging enough for someone without Keller's impairments. She could fall down the stairs or be bitten by an animal she didn't know was there. Helen could only feel her way around her environment.

In 1957, after learning to speak and write, and after becoming both a teacher and a humanitarian, Keller wrote in her book *The Open Door*, "Security is mostly a superstition. It does not exist in nature, nor do the children of men as a whole experience it. Avoiding danger is no safer in the long run than outright exposure. Life is either a daring adventure or nothing." She knew this because she had lived a life without safety or security and had become the person we know her to be because of it. She had lived a full life.

Keller was able to do this in part through her own incredible efforts and in part due to the community around her. Abraham Maslow argues in his hierarchy of needs that security and safety are the foundations that help an individual reach their full potential. Had Keller's teacher, Anne Sullivan, not been there to help her, she might not have lived up to her full potential. Formal sign language wasn't invented until 1620, and Braille wasn't created until 1824. Louis Braille would not have been able to invent his written language of embossed paper had he not been educated in Paris's Institut National des Jeunes Aveugles (National Institute for Blind Children). Alone, none of us can achieve as much as we can accomplish together.

I think Keller is right that security doesn't exist naturally. Cybersecurity, if and when it exists, exists precisely because it is man-made. Security requires you and me and everyone around us to participate in creating it. We are compelled to try because it makes us who we are: fathers, mothers, caretakers, friends, colleagues. Security gives us purpose and makes us a part of our community. Security frees us to live up to our potential. Security is not guaranteed, and the security our communities make is not perfect. But this desire to protect one another is part of what it means to be human.

When I was a kid, I recall having a conversation with my dad about some problem I was having. I was probably five years old. My dad told me that there are two ways of learning from a problem: the easy way and the hard way. The hard way was to tackle the problem myself, figure things out as I went, and make mistakes along the way. The easy way was to watch other people and learn the lessons from them as they learned the hard way. My dad was former Army Special Forces and had spent much of his career in Army Intelligence, so I can only imagine him learning his own lessons as he went along.

As I wrote this book, I interviewed security leaders and practitioners in almost every industry. One of the most important things for this book was telling the stories of the people in the security industry. In security, we play our cards close to the vest, meaning we don't like to talk about our stories out in the open. We do this for good reasons. Many of the individuals I talked to can't talk about their stories because the nondisclosure agreements or confidentiality provisions in contracts keep those stories from being told. But there's also concern about what would happen if the general public knew all the gory details of what happens in the battle to keep their information safe. The challenge with this is that by not sharing our stories, we can't collectively learn the lessons everyone has to teach us. Collectively, we're learning the hard way instead of the easy way.

Recently, I gave a keynote speech at a conference, and someone asked me what the most important cybersecurity habit is. All of these habits are important. But the person continued, if we must improve on just one of the habits, which one should we start on first? Maybe you have a natural gift of skepticism. Maybe you're already in a great culture. But if you're weak at one of the habits, which one should you focus on improving for the most immediate result?

We have a society for mutual protection. We come together to protect one another. And, as leaders, our highest calling is to protect our communities. We fail when we're disconnected.

Having read this book makes you part of a community.

Community is the most important of the nine habits. A security community is a collaboration between a league of community members to protect their common interests. Because security requires a community, and communities arrange themselves in hierarchies, different relationships tend to form with different security implications. In a family, you have your superiors (parents), you have your peers (siblings), you have your subordinates (children), and you have outsiders (friends and neighbors). What role you play in security varies depending on the relationship. In business, these same four relationships apply: You have a boss and coworkers, while some have subordinates, and there are outsiders like vendors or customers. A supervisor establishes the tone of the relationship by setting the example and creating the rules (written or unwritten) the organization will follow. Peers follow the tone set by the top, perhaps sharing information freely and collaborating, or keeping information close to the vest and functioning independently, as is dictated by the culture of the organization. Subordinates tend to adopt the culture of the organization they are in, or they leave, only rarely openly rebelling against that culture.

It's worth mentioning these four different types of community relationships because to successfully change security behaviors means different things depending on the relationship. As a part of the process of reading this book, you should choose one person from each category, either inside your family or at your office, and tell them you're reading this book. They can read this book with you, or you can tell them about it as you come across ideas that could benefit your community. Let them know you're going to try some different behaviors as you go through it and you'd like to get their feedback. How do the changes in your behavior affect them? Does their behavior change in response? My prediction is that the changes you make will have an impact on your four community members, and when they also begin to change, there will be a multiplier effect as small improvements ripple through your shared community. The requirements for this are communication and trust, even if only within a small inner circle. The more openly you discuss security, the greater the impact you will make.

NOTES

Introduction

1. **people are the cause:** Suzanne Widup et al., 2018 Verizon Data Breach Investigations Report, 2018.

2. **stress can shut down:** Carmen Sandi, "Stress and Cognition," Wiley Interdisciplinary Reviews: Cognitive Science 4, no. 3 (2013): 245–61, https://doi.org/10.1002/wcs.1222

3. **habits can't be thrown out:** Mark Twain, *The Tragedy of Pudd'nhead Wilson: And the Comedy Those Extraordinary Twins* (Hartford, CT: American Pub. Co., 1894).

Chapter 1

1. **smartphone at age ten:** "The Average Age for a Child Getting Their First Smartphone Is Now 10.3 Years," TechCrunch (blog), accessed June 18, 2019, http://social.techcrunch.com/2016/05/19/the-average-age-for-a-child-getting-their-first-smartphone-is-now-10-3-years/.

2. **Acevedo began her career:** "Meet Sylvia Acevedo, the Rocket Scientist in Charge of the Girl Scouts," CNN, accessed June 18, 2019, https://money.cnn.com/2017/05/19/news/girl-scouts-new-ceo/index.html.

3. **the concept of agile:** "What Is Agile Software Development?," *Agile Alliance* (blog), June 29, 2015, https://www.agilealliance.org/agile101/.

4.   **test anxiety:** "Test Anxiety: Why It Is Increasing and 3 Ways to Curb It," *Washington Post*, February 10, 2013, https://www.washingtonpost.com/news /answer-sheet/wp/2013/02/10/test-anxiety-why-it-is-increasing-and-3-ways -to-curb-it.

5.   **Controls for Effective Cyber Defense:** "CIS Controls," CIS, accessed June 18, 2019, https://www.cisecurity.org/controls/.

6.   **The kill chain:** "Cyber Kill Chain," Lockheed Martin, accessed June 18, 2019, https://www.lockheedmartin.com/en-us/capabilities/cyber/cyber-kill-chain .html.

7.   **no one was wiser:** Plato, *The Trial and Death of Socrates: Euthyphro, Apology, Crito, Death Scene from Phaedo*, 3rd ed., trans. George Maximilian Anthony Grube (Hackett Publishing, 2000).

8.   **Of my 57 years:** I.A Horowitz and Fred Reinfeld, *Chess Traps, Pitfalls and Swindles* (New York: Simon & Schuster, 1993).

9.   **The tapper was asked to:** Elizabeth Louise Newton, *The Rocky Road from Actions to Intentions*, 1990, https://searchworks.stanford.edu/view/508033.

10.   **The difficulty of our present:** Mike Massimino, *Spaceman: An Astronaut's Unlikely Journey to Unlock the Secrets of the Universe* (Crown Archetype 2016).

11.   **Who you gonna call:** "Privacy and Security," Federal Trade Commission, accessed June 18, 2019, https://www.ftc.gov/tips-advice/business-center /privacy-and-security.

12.   **You heard it here first:** "Google Alerts — Monitor the Web for Interesting New Content," Google, accessed June 18, 2019, https://www.google.com /alerts.

13.   **headline news:** Krebs on Security, accessed June 18, 2019, https:// krebsonsecurity.com/.

14.   **triune brain:** Paul D. MacLean, *The Triune Brain in Evolution: Role in Paleocerebral Functions* (New York; London: Plenum Press, 1990).

15.   **six primary emotions:** P. Ekman and W.V. Friesen, "Constants across Cultures in the Face and Emotion," *Journal of Personality and Social Psychology* 17, no. 2 (February 1971): 124–29.

16. **Brains are lazy:** Daniel Kahneman, *Thinking, Fast and Slow* (New York: Farrar, Straus and Giroux, 2011).

17. **advertisements on Facebook:** Scott Shane, "These Are the Ads Russia Bought on Facebook in 2016," *The New York Times*, November 1, 2017, sec. U.S., https://www.nytimes.com/2017/11/01/us/politics/russia-2016-election -facebook.html.

Chapter 2

1. **CEO of Texas Instruments:** "Texas Instruments Passes Over Two in Picking Chief," The New York Times, accessed June 19, 2019, https://www.nytimes .com/1996/06/21/business/texas-instruments-passes-over-two-in-picking-chief.html.

2. **protections within your network:** John Kindervag, "Build Security Into Your Network's DNA: The Zero Trust Network Architecture," *Forrester*, November 5, 2010, http://www.virtualstarmedia.com/downloads/Forrester_zero_trust _DNA.pdf.

3. **flexible alternative:** "No More Chewy Centers: The Zero Trust Model of Information Security," Forrester, 2016, https://www.forrester.com/report/ No+More+Chewy+Centers+The+Zero+Trust+Model+Of+Information+ Security/-/E-RES56682.

4. **When they first met:** "Suzanne Massie Taught President Ronald Reagan This Important Russian Phrase: 'Trust, but Verify,'" Public Radio International, accessed June 19, 2019, https://www.pri.org/stories/2014-03-07/suzanne -massie-taught-president-ronald-reagan-important-russian-phrase-trust.

5. **effect of researchers' expectations:** Robert Rosenthal and Kermit L. Fode, "The Effect of Experimenter Bias on the Performance of the Albino Rat," *Behavioral Science* 8, no. 3 (1963): 183–89, https://doi.org/10.1002 /bs.3830080302.

6. **above-average gains:** Robert Rosenthal and Lenore Jacobson, *Pygmalion in the Classroom: Teacher Expectation and Pupil's Intellectual Development* (Carmarthen, UK: Crown House, 2003).

7.   **human error:** Frank Ohlhorst, "IBM Says Most Security Breaches Are Due to Human Error," TechRepublic, accessed June 19, 2019, https://www .techrepublic.com/article/ibm-says-most-security-breaches-are-eue-to -human-error/.

8.   **Social engineers:** Kevin D. Mitnick and William L. Simon, *The Art of Deception: Controlling the Human Element of Security* (Indianapolis, IN: Wiley, 2002).

9.   **When trust is missing:** Stephen M.R. Covey and Rebecca R. Merrill, *The Speed of Trust: The One Thing That Changes Everything* (Free Press 2018).

10.   **Doubt is the heart:** Rabbi Eric H. Yoffie, "Doubt Is the Heart of Belief," HuffPost, accessed June 19, 2019, https://www.huffpost.com/entry/doubt-is -the-heart-of-belief_b_3409838.

11.   **a memo to NASA:** "Remembering the Mistakes of Challenger," NASASpaceFlight.com, accessed June 19, 2019, https://www.nasaspaceflight .com/2007/01/remembering-the-mistakes-of-challenger/.

12.   **going to blow up:** Sarah Kaplan, "Finally Free from Guilt over Challenger Disaster, an Engineer Dies in Peace," *Washington Post,* March 22, 2016, sec. Morning Mix, https://www.washingtonpost.com/news/morning-mix /wp/2016/03/22/finally-free-from-guilt-over-challenger-disaster-an -engineer-dies-in-peace/.

13.   **most famous fables:** http://read.gov/aesop/043.html.

14.   **In October 2007:** Meredith Whitney and Carla Krawiec, "Is Citigroup's Dividend Safe? Downgrading Stock Due to Capital Concerns," The New York Times (blog), October 31, 2007, http://graphics7.nytimes.com/images /blogs/dealbook/Citi_report_CIBC.pdf.

15.   **According to:** Michael Lewis, *The Big Short: Inside the Doomsday Machine* (W.W. Norton & Co. 2010).

16.   **when taking risks:** Susan Cain, *Quiet: The Power of Introverts in a World That Can't Stop Talking* (London: Penguin Books, 2013).

17.   **geared to respond:** John Brebner and Christopher Cooper, "A Proposed Unified Model of Extraversion," *Motivation, Emotion, and Personality*, 1985, 219–229.

18.   **forum for healthy debate:** *NASA Technical Reports Server (NTRS) 20100030545: Success Legacy of the Space Shuttle Program: Changes in Shuttle Post Challenger and Columbia*, NASA, 2010, http://archive.org/details /NASA_NTRS_Archive_20100030545.

Chapter 3

1.   **focal point:** "The Origin of 'Where's Waldo,'" Today I Found Out, August 30, 2013, http://www.todayifoundout.com/index.php/2013/08/the-history-of -wheres-waldo/.

2.   **defeated Waldo-searchers:** "Here's Waldo: Computing the Optimal Search Strategy for Finding Waldo," *Dr. Randal S. Olson* (blog), February 3, 2015, http://www.randalolson.com/2015/02/03/heres-waldo-computing-the -optimal-search-strategy-for-finding-waldo/.

3.   **only have to be lucky once:** Peter Taylor, *The War against the IRA* (London: Bloomsbury Publishing PLC : [distributor] Macmillan Distribution [MDL], 2002).

4.   **read cartoons taken:** Fritz Strack, Leonard L. Martin, and Sabine Stepper, "Inhibiting and Facilitating Conditions of the Human Smile: A Nonobtrusive Test of the Facial Feedback Hypothesis," *Journal of Personality and Social Psychology* 54, no. 5 (1988): 768.

5.   **Psychologists believe frowning:** Andreas Hennenlotter et al., "The Link between Facial Feedback and Neural Activity within Central Circuitries of Emotion—New Insights from Botulinum Toxin–Induced Denervation of Frown Muscles," *Cerebral Cortex* 19, no. 3 (March 1, 2009): 537–42, https:// doi.org/10.1093/cercor/bhn104.

6.   **moonwalking bear:** Tracy McVeigh, "Invisible Bear Makes Cyclists Safer," The Guardian, November 15, 2008, https://www.theguardian.com/uk/2008 /nov/16/transport-invisible-bear-cyclists-youtube.

7.   **given a complex task:** Cal Newport, Deep Work (London: Piatkus, 2016).

8.   **$2 billion in 2016:** "FBI Warns of Dramatic Increase in Business E-Mail Scams," Press Release, Federal Bureau of Investigation, accessed June 20, 2019, https://www.fbi.gov/contact-us/field-offices/phoenix/news/press -releases/fbi-warns-of-dramatic-increase-in-business-e-mail-scams.

9.   **Our cognitive abilities:** Daniel H. Pink, *When: The Scientific Secrets of Perfect Timing* (New York: Penguin, 2019).

10.   **legal limit of alcohol:** Russell G. Foster and Leon Kreitzman, *Rhythms of Life: The Biological Clocks That Control the Daily Lives of Every Living Thing* (New Haven, CT: Yale University Press, 2005)

11.   **nature of that task:** Simon Folkard, "Diurnal Variation in Locical Reasoning," *British Journal of Psychology* 66, no. 1 (1975).

12.   **Researchers placed subjects:** Paul J. Whalen and Elizabeth A. Phelps, *The Human Amygdala* (New York: Guilford Press, 2009).

13.   **eight-week course:** Adrienne A. Taren, J. David Creswell, and Peter J. Gianaros, "Dispositional Mindfulness Co-Varies with Smaller Amygdala and Caudate Volumes in Community Adults," *PLOS ONE* 8, no. 5 (May 22, 2013): e64574, https://doi.org/10.1371/journal.pone.0064574.

Chapter 4

1.   **In 2000:** United States of America, Appellee v. Microsoft Corporation, Appellant, 253 F.3d 34 (D.C. Cir. 2001), Justia Law, accessed June 24, 2019, https://law.justia.com/cases/federal/appellate-courts/F3/253/34/576095/.

2.   **private detectives bribed:** Brad Stone, "Diving Into Bill's Trash," Newsweek, July 9, 2000, https://www.newsweek.com/diving-bills-trash-161599.

3.   **leaked US diplomatic cables:** Guardian Staff, "US Embassy Cables: China Uses Access to Microsoft Source Code to Help Plot Cyber Warfare, US Fears," *The Guardian*, December 4, 2010, sec. Technology, https://www.theguardian.com/world/us-embassy-cables-documents/214462.

4.   **computers in Ukraine:** Sheera Frenkel, Mark Scott, and Paul Mozur, "Mystery of Motive for a Ransomware Attack: Money, Mayhem or a Message?," *The New York Times*, June 28, 2017, sec. Business, https://www.nytimes.com/2017/06/28/business/ramsonware-hackers-cybersecurity-petya-impact.html.

5.   **accidentally:** "The Untold Story of NotPetya, the Most Devastating Cyberattack in History," *Wired*, August 22, 2018, https://www.wired.com/story/notpetya-cyberattack-ukraine-russia-code-crashed-the-world/.

6. **Thomas sold his:** "Thomas Edison and Menlo Park" The Thomas Edison
    Center at Menlo Park, accessed June 20, 2019, http://www
    .menloparkmuseum.org/history/thomas-edison-and-menlo-park/.

7. **lab-specific notebooks:** "The Invention Factory: Year of Innovation Series,"
    The Edison Papers, Rutgers School of Arts and Sciences, accessed June 22,
    2019, http://edison.rutgers.edu/inventionfactory.htm.

8. **Jobs's fear came true:** John C. Abell, "Jan. 19, 1983: Apple Gets Graphic
    With Lisa," *Wired*, January 19, 2010, https://www.wired
    .com/2010/01/0119apple-unveils-lisa/.

9. **In his biography:** Walter Isaacson, *Steve Jobs* (New York: Simon and Schuster,
    2011).

10. **leaked details online:** Jesus Diaz, "How Apple Lost the iPhone 4," Gizmodo,
    April 19, 2010, https://gizmodo.com/how-apple-lost-the-iphone-4-5520438.

11. **staying late:** Melissa Chan, "Bill Gates Memorized Employees' License
    Plates to Track Them at Work," *Time*, February 1, 2016, https://time
    .com/4202737/bill-gates-license-plates-employees/.

12. **He was also the creator:** David Greelish, "An Interview with Computing
    Pioneer Alan Kay," *Time*, accessed June 24, 2019, http://techland.time
    .com/2013/04/02/an-interview-with-computing-pioneer-alan-kay/.

13. **The local paper:** "A Brief Biography of Thomas Edison," Thomas Edison
    National Historical Park (U.S. National Park Service), accessed June 22, 2019,
    https://www.nps.gov/edis/learn/kidsyouth/a-brief-biography-of-thomas
    -edison.htm.

14. **wants to change your mind:** Adam Shostack, *Threat Modeling: Designing for
    Security* (Indianapolis, IN: John Wiley & Sons, 2014).

15. **data breach investigation:** Kellman Meghu, "How NOT to Do Security—
    Lessons Learned from the Galactic Empire—SecTor 2012," Vimeo, accessed
    June 24, 2019, http://2012.video.sector.ca/video/51119497.

Chapter 5

1. **The psychologist's name:** R.I.M. Dunbar, "Neocortex Size as a Constraint on Group Size in Primates," *Journal of Human Evolution* 22, no. 6 (June 1, 1992): 469–93, https://doi.org/10.1016/0047-2484(92)90081-J.

2. **Once humans developed:** Charles Gross, "Alfred Russell Wallace and the Evolution of the Human Mind," *The Neuroscientist* 16, no. 5 (October 2010): 496–507, https://doi.org/10.1177/1073858410377236.

3. **To borrow a quote:** Alexander Graydon, *Memoirs of His Own Time: With Reminiscences of the Men and Events of the Revolution* (Lindsay & Blakiston, 1846).

4. **diverse companies:** Vivian Hunt et al., "Delivering Growth through Diversity in the Workplace," McKinsey, accessed June 27, 2019, https://www .mckinsey.com/business-functions/organization/our-insights/delivering-through-diversity.

5. **But once wasn't:** M.E.P. Seligman, "Learned Helplessness," *Annual Review of Medicine* 23, no. 1 (February 1, 1972): 407–12, https://doi.org/10.1146 /annurev.me.23.020172.002203.

6. **random acts of kindness:** Sonja Lyubomirsky, Kennon M. Sheldon, and David Schkade, "Pursuing Happiness: The Architecture of Sustainable Change," *Review of General Psychology* 9, no. 2 (2005): 111–131.

7. **Willpower isn't just a skill:** Charles Duhigg, *The Power of Habit: Why We Do What We Do in Life and Business* (Doubleday Canada, 2012).

8. **wash their hands:** Ahmet Doğan Ataman, Emine Elif Vatanoğlu-Lutz, and Gazi Yıldırım, "Medicine in Stamps-Ignaz Semmelweis and Puerperal Fever," *Journal of the Turkish German Gynecological Association* 14, no. 1 (March 1, 2013): 35–39, https://doi.org/10.5152/jtgga.2013.08.

9. **compliance rate:** D. Pittet, "Improving Adherence to Hand Hygiene Practice: A Multidisciplinary Approach," Emerging Infectious Diseases Journal — CDC 7, no. 2 (April 2001), accessed April, 2020, https://www .ncbi.nlm.nih.gov/pmc/articles/PMC2631736/pdf/11294714.pdf.

10. **how much soap:** Adam M. Grant and David A. Hofmann, "It's Not All About Me: Motivating Hand Hygiene Among Health Care Professionals

by Focusing on Patients," *Psychological Science* 22, no. 12 (December 1, 2011): 1494–99, https://doi.org/10.1177/0956797611419172.

11.   **rats ran the maze:** "How the Brain Controls Our Habits," MIT News, accessed June 27, 2019, http://news.mit.edu/2012/understanding-how -brains-control-our-habits-1029.

12.   **remnants of the Morris worm:** "The Morris Worm. 30 Years Since First Major Attack on the Internet," FBI, accessed March 1, 2020, https://www .fbi.gov/news/stories/morris-worm-30-years-since-first-major-attack-on -internet-110218.

13.   **spawned a series of:** Stuart McClure, Joel Scambray, and George Kurtz, *Hacking Exposed 7: Network Security Secrets and Solutions* (McGraw Hill Professional, 2012).

14.   **$1.4 billion:** https://www.blackberry.com/us/en/company/newsroom/press -releases/2018/blackberry-acquisition-press-release.

Chapter 6

1.   **After three months:** Sheina Orbell et al., "Self-Efficacy and Goal Importance in the Prediction of Physical Disability in People Following Hospitalization: A Prospective Study," *British Journal of Health Psychology* 6, no. 1 (2001): 25–40, https://doi.org/10.1348/135910701169034.

2.   **CEO of IBM:** Edgar H. Schein, *Organizational Culture and Leadership* (San Francisco: Jossey-Bass [Wiley Imprint], 2006).

3.   **The story sparked:** "Our Lady of the Angels School Fire: 50 Years Later," Fire Engineering, accessed July 5, 2019 [subscription-based], https://www .fireengineering.com/articles/print/volume-161/issue-12/features/our-lady-of -the-angels-school-fire-50-years-later.html.

4.   **training scars:** Lt. Col. Dave Grossman and Loren Christensen, *On Combat: The Psychology and Physiology of Deadly Conflict in War and in Peace* (BookBaby, 2017).

5.   **He didn't abduct:** "How the Tylenol Murders of 1982 Changed the Way We Consume Medication," PBS NewsHour, September 29, 2014, https://www .pbs.org/newshour/health/tylenol-murders-1982.

Chapter 7

1. **hierarchy of needs:** A.H. Maslow, "A Theory of Human Motivation," *Psychological Review* 50, no. 4 (1943): 370–96, https://doi.org/10.1037/h0054346.

2. **security has a poverty line:** Warwick Ashford, "Industry Needs to Address Security Poverty Line, Says Analyst," *Computer Weekly*, April 22, 2013, https://www.computerweekly.com/news/2240182139/Industry-needs-to-address-security-poverty-line-says-analyst.

3. **Friends hold a mirror:** Massimo Pigliucci, *Answers for Aristotle: How Science and Philosophy Can Lead Us to A More Meaningful Life* (Basic Books, 2012).

Chapter 8

1. **When he took:** G. di Pellegrino et al., "Understanding Motor Events: A Neurophysiological Study," *Experimental Brain Research* 91, no. 1 (October 1, 1992): 176–80, https://doi.org/10.1007/BF00230027.

2. **mirror neurons:** Marco Iacoboni et al., "Grasping the Intentions of Others with One's Own Mirror Neuron System," *PLOS Biology* 3, no. 3 (February 22, 2005): e79, https://doi.org/10.1371/journal.pbio.0030079.

3. **exquisitely social creatures:** Sandra Blakeslee, "Cells That Read Minds," *The New York Times*, January 10, 2006, sec. Health, https://www.nytimes.com/2006/01/10/science/cells-that-read-minds.html.

4. **Tolstoy once wrote:** Leo Tolstoy, *Pamphlets. Translated from the Russian* (Christchurch, Hants., Free Age Press, 1900), http://archive.org/details/pamphletstransl00tolsgoog.

5. **resources for self-understanding:** Carl Ransom Rogers, *The Carl Rogers Reader* (Houghton Mifflin Harcourt, 1989).

6. **what you see is all there is:** Kahneman, *Thinking, Fast and Slow*.

7. **360-degree feedback:** Marshall Goldsmith, *What Got You Here Won't Get You There: How Successful People Become Even More Successful* (Profile Books, 2010).

Chapter 9

1. **Lance worked with:** "The Honeynet Project: Whitepapers," The Honeynet Project, accessed July 6, 2019, https://www.honeynet.org/papers/.

2. **creative spark:** *Feist Publications, Inc., Petitioner v. Rural Telephone Service Company, Inc.*, 499 U.S. 340 (111 S.Ct. 1282, 113 L.Ed.2d 358).

3. **Houdini:** William Kalush and Larry Sloman, *The Secret Life of Houdini: The Making of America's First Superhero* (Simon & Schuster, 2006).

INDEX

ABOUT THE AUTHOR

George Finney is a chief information security officer who believes that people are the key to solving our cybersecurity challenges. George has worked in cybersecurity for nearly twenty years and has helped startups, global telecommunications firms, and nonprofits improve their security posture. As part of his passion for education, George has taught cybersecurity at Southern Methodist University and is the author of several cybersecurity books, including *No More Magic Wands: Transformative Cybersecurity Change for Everyone*. George has been recognized by Security magazine as one of its top cybersecurity leaders in 2018, and he is part of the Texas CISO Council, a member of the board of directors of the Palo Alto Networks FUEL User Group, and an advisory board member for SecureWorld. George holds a Juris Doctor degree from Southern Methodist University and a Bachelor of Arts from St. John's College, as well as multiple cybersecurity certifications, including the CISSP, CISM, and CIPP.